Product-Line Strategies

Edited by Earl L. Bailey

A Report from The Conference Board

Contents

About This Report

THIS REPORT examines practical issues and options that managements face in developing market strategy for their companies' product lines. It is divided into three parts. Part I deals with fundamental frameworks for product-line strategy. Parts II and III look separately at planning prospects and requirements on behalf of products and lines intended, respectively, for consumer markets or for industrial markets. (While the focus and concerns of these disparate planning missions often differ in some respects, many of the observations and pointers found in these two sections of the report clearly have application within both settings.)

The report's various chapters, created originally for presentation at recent programs of The Conference Board, include numerous examples and guidelines from a group of experienced practitioners exceptionally well positioned to provide them. The Conference Board is grateful to these contributors, listed on the opposite page, for their cooperation in this venture. Their presentations have been edited for publication by Earl L. Bailey, the Board's Director of Marketing Management Research.

The Contributors

Linden A. Davis, Jr.
Senior Vice President and
  Director of Research
McCaffrey and McCall, Inc.

Richard O. Donegan
Senior Vice President and
  Group Executive
General Electric Company

Rodman L. Drake
Managing Director
Cresap, McCormick and Paget Inc.

John L. Forbis
Principal
McKinsey & Company

Samuel R. Gardner
Vice President — Marketing
Retail Food Group
Kraft Inc.

Bruce J. Hoesman
Vice President — Planning
  and Business Development
American Hospital Supply Corporation

Kent B. Monroe
Head, Department of Marketing
Virginia Polytechnic Institute
  and State University

William T. Moran
President
Moran, Inc.

Albert G. Munkelt
Senior Vice President —
  Marketing Planning
Foods Division
The Coca-Cola Company

John W. Peterson
Divisional Vice President
  and General Manager
Diamond Products Division
Norton Company

Thomas W. Peterson
Vice President — Marketing
Vick Europe/Africa Division
Richardson-Vicks Inc.

John R. Rhode
Vice President — Marketing
  and Planning
Industrial Products Group
Combustion Engineering, Inc.

David B. Smart
Director
Food Enterprises Division
Ralston Purina Company

George M. Zapp
Vice President—Planning
  and Development
Chemicals Group
PPG Industries, Inc.

Introduction and Summary

Earl L. Bailey
Director, Marketing
Management Research
The Conference Board, Inc.

THE CREATION OF STRATEGY is a prerequisite for guiding the successful marketing of a product, a brand, or a service—or lines of related offerings. This prior matching of marketing means and ends calls for considerable imagination and insight on the part of the marketer. With good reason, the task has been likened to that confronting the military strategist.

There is, of course, an implied strategy underlying any action by a combatant—in the marketplace or on the field of battle. But strategy that ensures highly *relevant* direction for an entire campaign is not something easily improvised on the spot. On his own success as a strategist, even Napoleon was forced to acknowledge: "It is not some unfamiliar spirit which suddenly discloses to me what I have to do in a case unexpected by others; it is a reflection, a meditation."

Opportunities for similar meditation are by now built routinely into the marketing planning procedures of a growing number of companies.[1] Thus, among marketers generally, there is stronger preference nowadays than ever for the careful, systematic formulation of strategy to guide future marketing efforts. At the same time, many marketing planners have come to rely more heavily on a number of formal planning tools, including principles and analytical devices borrowed in recent years from the expanding kit of the corporate planner.

Within the company, several factors have frequently reinforced this new stress on a disciplined approach to the establishment of market strategy. Among the most common are:

- Growing insistence—in marketing and in other functional areas of the company—on an orderly marshaling of facts, gauging of risks, and weighing of alternatives before final commitment to action.
- Insistence, too, that individual product strategies be fashioned to support goals established at higher levels or for broader aggregations within the planning hierarchy—for example, for an entire operating unit, for a strategic business unit, or for the company as a whole.
- A closer review of proposed product strategies in advance—by senior marketing management and by general management—in companies where some elements of the planning job have been routinely delegated to product managers or others in middle management.
- Increased recognition that the specific combination of competing brands or even generic product types defining "*the* market" for a given brand or product line of the company is not always self-evident or readily ascertainable; with further recognition, however, that strategic choices may be flawed unless the problem of defining market boundaries is satisfactorily resolved.
- Perception, as well, that broad, generalized strategies—such as for growth or for product proliferation—cannot safely be applied across the board for all product lines in the multiproduct company, since appropriate strategy choices in each case depend logically upon competitive circumstances and other factors unique to that particular offering.
- Widespread urgings, nonetheless, that strategies for different product lines be reinforcing and compatible, insofar as this is possible.

The chapters to follow examine a number of important implications of these developments for the marketing strategist.

---

[1]See, for example, David S. Hopkins, *The Marketing Plan*. The Conference Board, Report No. 801, 1981.

A New Planning Environment

Abundant evidence in recent years confirms that, even with senior management actively promoting the cause, it takes time to convert "strategic planning" from a buzzword to a watchword throughout the company. During the process, managers at all levels and in all functions are usually compelled to focus intensively on planning questions and linkages beyond those narrowly associated with the areas of direct concern to them. Oftentimes, they find that working in a strategy-oriented environment requires some readjustment of their customary thinking and procedures.

In this connection, Richard O. Donegan, Senior Vice President and Group Executive of General Electric Company asserts that, for companies' marketing efforts to be truly strategy-based, marketers hereafter will have to move beyond reliance on traditional forms of environmental scanning, market segmentation, and competitive monitoring. As Mr. Donegan sees it, for example, the strategy-oriented marketing of the future will require a shift from mere scanning of the environment to more penetrating environmental analyses. Further, an awareness of the simple demographics that may be associated with different segments in a market will become less important, he asserts, than the identification of competitive leverage points for the company. Marketers, in his opinion, will also need to project the probable actions of competitors; and, to play it safe, they will have to rely more heavily in the future on contingency planning.

Fortunately, today's marketing planners have more resources on which to draw than did their predecessors in laying the strategic foundations for marketing action. These resources include access to a number of planning aids, constructs and disciplines which have been popularized over the past decade. George M. Zapp, Vice President—Planning and Development for the Chemicals Group of PPG Industries, singles out for illustration four such concepts in current use. Each offers specialized assumptions and methodologies for diagnosing the seller's competitive situation and possibilities for making strategic moves. The four include: the strategic planning grid; the product life-cycle planning system; the application of experience curve theory to market analysis; and the PIMS (Profit Impact of Market Strategy) data bank.

Tools like these, in Mr. Zapp's experience, offer business planners a potentially valuable starting point in setting strategy. Although they are not equally applicable in all product/market situations, he is convinced that "wise managements will encourage the continued exploring of such strategic disciplines."

Many variants of planning tools like these are now in use. According to John Rhode, Vice President—Marketing and Planning of Combustion Engineering's Industrial Products Group, one that is especially favored by his company is the "maturity-cycle," a concept applied in the course of planning on behalf of a business, a product line, an individual product, or even a grouping of customers. Explaining that strategy choices and priorities necessarily differ in each case, Mr. Rhode stresses this basic theme: "Objectives, strategies and tactics formulated for a line must be consistent with each other and with the state of relative maturity of the market." And he suggests that managers must go out of their way to put themselves in competitors' shoes—to see what reactions their proposed actions might be expected to trigger on the part of the company's competitors.

Consumer Markets

Many of the principles of planning have proved applicable in a variety of marketing situations. In the case of a particular product line, of course, the mix of strategic options necessarily reflects both company and market considerations unique to that line. The concerns of different planners tend to be least similar where product markets under review are unlike in fundamental ways—as between markets made up of individual consumers and those made up of industrial or business users. For instance, planners on behalf of consumer branded items are often forced to emphasize issues and distinctions involving product categories, product lines, and brands, which are judged to have considerable strategic importance in their specialized markets.

There are several means by which enterprising marketers of consumer goods discover and take advantage of new competitive opportunities. For example, David B. Smart, Director of the Food Enterprises Division of Ralston Purina Company, identifies the following as possibilities: altering media strategy; capitalizing on promising opportunities for product positioning; refurbishing an existing product's profile; finding new niches in the marketplace; ensuring meaningful product differences; uncovering alternative distribution methods; extending the product line with new forms or varieties; providing additional advantages through packaging; and adapting to new demographic changes. In all of this, he says, an approach to marketing action that is realistic and properly timed can be critical. So, too, can be a continuing belief in and search for "a better way."

For consumer product planners, the possibility of attaining strategic objectives through extensions to an existing product line often has strong appeal. This is especially so, explains Thomas W. Peterson, Vice President—Marketing, Vick Europe/Africa Division of Richardson-Vicks, Inc., for marketers who face a proliferation of competing brands in their markets and, as a result, drastic increases in the costs of capturing consumer attention.

He cites a number of potential advantages to introducing new items under the protection of an established brand umbrella. But he also warns of potential dangers awaiting those who diffuse or misuse a brand's image through inappropriate extensions to the line. Referring to recent examples supporting the point, Mr. Peterson makes this observation: "At the heart of every successful product-line marketing strategy is the recognition that the brand name must connote some kind of specific consumer benefit, and that benefit must be the same across all products in the line."

The breadth and depth of the product line are matters of natural, continuing concern to those responsible for its welfare. Drawing on examples from the food industry, Albert C. Munkelt, Senior Vice President—Marketing Planning of Coca-Cola's Food Division, shows why the optimum number and mix of offerings in each case depend on factors related to the brand or trademark in question, including "the limitations of the particular product category, the financial and technical resources of the manufacturer, the company's marketing skill or strategy, and the brand's consumer acceptance."

The same executive goes on to offer several rules of thumb for deciding on whether to extend a line. He recommends, for example, that every extension promise additional profit for the brand or line, as well as an enhancement of its image. The extension should also enjoy credibility with the consumer. Yet another critical question is whether retailers will "authorize" the company's proposed line extension and welcome it on their shelves.

When it comes to the positioning of a brand in the market, the final determinant, of course, is not simply the manufacturer's strategic hopes or intentions. From his vantage point in a major advertising agency, Linden A. Davis, Jr., Senior Vice President and Director of Research, of McCaffrey and McCall, Inc., confirms that what counts most is the consumer's perception of the brand, since "positioning is really a state of mind."

In fact, how consumers perceptually position a brand may differ in important ways from the seller's original expectations. Such was the case, Mr. Davis suggests, with Colgate's Irish Spring soap, although the outcome in this case proved fortuitous for the seller. A marketer's best route to positioning, he believes, is to start with an open mind, disregarding all prior assumptions about the product category being considered.

Research can provide valuable guidance by showing how, when and where competing brands—or product categories themselves—are being used by consumers. In the opinion of Mr. Davis, it is only as a final step after a thorough study of consumer behavior that an appropriate position can be targeted for the brand.

One manufacturer with an impressive mix of consumer-market positioning possibilities and solutions is Kraft Inc. (part of Dart & Kraft, Inc.). According to the Vice President—Marketing of Kraft's Retail Food Group, Samuel R. Gardner, the company has followed a segmented-positioning path, which calls for an offering

of multiple brands within each of several different product categories.

In the highly competitive ice cream category, for example, Kraft elected to follow a three-brand strategy. The challenge, as outlined by Mr. Gardner, was to find ways of positioning Kraft's regional Breyers brand as a national premium product in markets where the company was already represented by its Sealtest brand, and then eventually to launch an ice milk product as well to those same markets under the Light n' Lively name.

The research, planning and promotional efforts supporting this multibrand strategy, described by Mr. Gardner, paid off in consumer and trade acceptance for what ultimately was to become a broad line of packaged frozen desserts. Since then, he relates, Kraft has proceeded to apply similar positioning principles to other product categories.

In any company, the various strategy decisions made by marketing management may call for some critical trade-offs. In the opinion of William Moran, President of Moran, Inc., future choices of this kind will be strongly influenced by the impact of a firm's proposed actions on its ability to remain cost-competitive—relative to both direct and indirect competitors. He goes on to show that "the repeat purchase rate for a product category"—an analog for market concentration—"offers a quick and easy way to screen potential new categories for their relative attractiveness."

Mr. Moran further demonstrates the usefulness of knowing a product's "substitutability"—a measure that correlates with its marketing profit potential—as well as the value to the company of the product's repeat purchasers. Finally, for guiding the marketing planner toward the most profitable strategy choices, he proposes reliance on a "compound strategic model," which combines experience-curve and marketing-related factors that are critical to success.

Industrial Markets

The company that serves nonconsumer markets, no less than the marketer of consumer items, must, of course, link its marketing effort realistically to the interests and requirements of product users. One consideration is the economic value of a product's purchase to the individual customer (EVC). "Ultimately," observes John L. Forbis, a principal of McKinsey & Company, "it is the economic value that we can deliver to the customer—and our ability to differentiate it from our competitor's offering—that promises us maximum leverage in terms of profitability."

In the case of an existing industrial product, its aggregate current cost to a buyer is the sum of the purchase price, the start-up costs, and the post-purchase costs for maintenance and operations. Armed with such information, explains Mr. Forbis, a marketer can apply the techniques of EVC analysis to develop appropriate pricing, segmentation and other marketing strategies, with at least the possibility of changing the competitive game to the company's advantage and thus avoiding costly head-on competition.

Again, like manufacturers of consumer goods, producers of products destined for industrial and commercial use must decide on the mix of different product types and variations that each product line should encompass. If this mix is altered in some way, points out John W. Peterson, Divisional Vice President and General Manager of Norton Company's Diamond Products Division, it can affect overall sales, other products in the line, the reactions of resellers and of competitors, and the costs incurred by the company for materials, manufacturing, selling or administration.

A logical starting point in dealing with these matters, he notes, is to review and define each of the company's separate businesses. Then, potential strategic options for individual product lines can be assayed. These may be found to include opportunities for exploiting a proprietary product or process; maintaining or expanding a large market share; capitalizing on a scarce or unique resource; identifying a defensible subsegment of the market; or using a "Number 2" market position to advantage. Decisions thereafter on the product types and variations for each line will need to be consistent with the underlying strategy that has been set for it.

When weighing a possible entry into a new market or the launching of an entirely new product or line, a company's management often needs help in evaluating the merits of the case. The business development model of the American Hospital Supply Corporation is an example of a tool designed for this purpose. As described by Bruce J. Hoesman, the company's Vice President—Planning and Business Development, this model consists of selected factors—some internal to the company and others external or market-related—which have probable bearing on the success of the proposed venture. Thus, the model takes into account such characteristics as the expected market potential, market share, cash flow, distribution strengths, and the like. Applying a system of judgmental weights and points to each factor, a management committee has been effective in identifying promising new directions for the company.

Often, one of the trickiest tasks in actually introducing a new product to the competitive market is establishing a logical price for it. According to one authority on pricing, Kent B. Monroe, head of the Department of Marketing at Virginia Polytechnic Institute and State University, too many industrial products firms have con-

tinued to rely naively on cost as the principal basis for setting prices, thus ignoring potentially valuable lessons from pricing research. He shows how value analysis, for example, can help to gauge buyers' perceived value of a new offering relative to their cost of acquiring it, and how such information can help in fashioning product and pricing strategies.

Among the common failings in new product pricing, Dr. Monroe cites management overeagerness in attempting to recover the company's investment too quickly. He then demonstrates how "contribution analysis" can facilitate sound pricing decisions. Underscoring further the potential payoff from research into pricing, Dr. Monroe offers this reminder: "The time to worry about market response to a price decision is before the decision has been made."

For those charged with the management of existing product lines, it might appear that countless opportunities exist for making critical trade-off decisions. But such is not the case, asserts Rodman L. Drake, Managing Director of Cresap, McCormick and Paget Inc. He points out that "the number of areas in which true strategic trade-offs are viable can quickly be reduced to a manageable number by separating structural constraints, or 'facts of life,' from variables over which management has direct or indirect influence." Like other contributors to this report, Mr. Drake is a strong advocate of "fact-based" strategy, which takes into account the key points of leverage and vulnerability for the company in the market.

Since market strategy on behalf of industrial products always depends on a number of functions besides marketing, he states that such strategy, therefore, is necessarily "linked to technological considerations, product design changes, changes in manufacturing costs, or improved service capabilities." As a result, in at least these respects, it often differs "from consumer marketing strategy, where product positioning, packaging, advertising and point-of-sale promotion are frequently key elements."

The important thing, as Mr. Drake sees it, is that the trade-off issues in marketing call, by definition, for the making of strategic choices. Therefore, they are always best approached not simply from the limited perspective of the marketing function, but rather from the broader perspective and concerns of general management. This one message, more than anything else, perhaps best summarizes recommendations made one way or another by virtually all of the contributors to this report. And there are signs that it also reflects a theme gaining increased emphasis recently within marketing-oriented companies of all kinds.

Part I

Frameworks for Product-Line Strategy

The Strategy-Oriented Marketing Effort

Richard O. Donegan
Senior Vice President and Group Executive
General Electric Company

THE CONSENSUS of leading futurists is that economic, social and political shifts of unprecedented magnitude lie ahead in America and in the world. Whatever else these changes portend for American business, the odds are favorable that they will usher in a full spectrum of new marketing opportunities brilliantly disguised as problems.

In an environment of accelerating change and intensifying world competition, it is unlikely that traditional marketing approaches will be adequate to identify and fully capitalize on these opportunities. Traditional marketing—which many businesses still use quite successfully—is rooted in the assumption that the world of the future will be very much like the world of the past, and that what has worked in the marketplace in the past—adjusted intuitively to accommodate slowly changing macrotrends and ad hoc discontinuities—will work again in the future.

In some businesses it will. But I believe that the majority of successful marketing operations in the future will take a strategy-oriented approach to the marketplace.

Strategic planning is a popular adolescent on the business scene. As a consequence, the term "strategy" is widely used—and often abused—as a description for nearly every type of plan, program and activity. Rather than discussing the term out of context, I would prefer to illustrate some of the elements of a strategy-oriented approach to the market and to contrast these with the elements of a more traditional marketing approach.

First, consider traditional marketing—and let me acknowledge that the shortcomings of this approach are being presented in hyperbole in order to differentiate clearly between traditional and strategy-oriented marketing. An abridged illustration of the traditional marketing process might appropriately include three familiar elements:

- Environmental scanning;
- Segmentation of consumer, customer and geographic markets; and
- Competitive monitoring.

Environmental Scanning

Environmental scanning is a process designed to identify high-probability macrotrends as a basis for developing business assumptions. Inflation, for example, would qualify as an obvious macrotrend that is likely to be with us for a long while to come. High price increases for energy are virtually guaranteed for at least the next decade, and this will give momentum to many other inflationary forces. This scan would consider a number of forecasts with respect to the probable rate of inflation and arrive at a consensus in the range of a 6 to 8 percent average annual rate for the next ten years.

Under a traditional approach, this assumption would then be cranked into marketing planning primarily in terms of its extrapolated impact on product costs and selling prices, and on the potential price/share trade-offs in contrast to those of competitors to maintain or increase the volume or profit margin. It is doubtful that the traditional approach would extend even these limited considerations much beyond the span of the current merchandising calendar or product-planning cycle—perhaps 18 to 36 months ahead.

Segmentation

Another element in the traditional process is market segmentation which, for sellers of consumer goods, appropriately embraces three submarkets—consumers, customers (i.e., retailers), and geographic markets.

Consumer segmentation, in a traditional approach, is

generally limited to surface demographics which, for example, indicate that:

- Birth rates are slowing;
- Life spans are increasing; and, therefore,
- The population is growing older.

At the outset of the 1980's, these observations corresponded to those published by a major magazine in a supplement which included a highlighted forecast that the "nation will grow older on average, forcing business and politics to woo more mature audiences." This bordered on the suggestion that there would be a dearth of new consumers in the 1980's. When considered in tandem with surface trends indicating slower growth rates in both real disposal income and household formations in that decade, this presented a rather pessimistic outlook for the consumer market.

Customer or trade-channel segmentation—in the retail market—is traditionally done by store classification: department stores, discount stores, hardware stores, and so forth. And traditional planning generally focuses on methods of concentrating marketing firepower on low-penetration store classifications. Differences between store classifications become increasingly obscure, however, as retailers expand the scope of their offerings by adding specialty sections to increase volume and working capital turnover.

Similarly, traditional geographic segmentation may identify low-penetration target markets, or needs for establishing or modifying distribution capabilities. It generally follows the design of population clusters—metropolitan vs. rural, zone vs. region, and so on.

Competitive Monitoring

To close the loop on the traditional marketing process, competitive monitoring is usually limited to developing a picture of what competitors have done or are doing, as reported in trade and business periodicals, in syndicated research reports, or through field personnel. More often than not, this kind of intelligence focuses on pricing and promotional tactics, product introductions, and distribution changes. Any deeper analysis tends to be product-line parochial, which obscures a competitor's total business strengths and vulnerabilities.

The traditional marketing approach just described is, by definition, attuned more to the past than to the future. Its tools are rudimentary and not suitable for digging much below the surface. Considering the anticipated dynamics and documented uncertainties ahead, a traditional marketing approach to the future might be likened to driving an Edsel in a Grand Prix race while blindfolded—and getting instructions from someone looking out the rear window.

The Strategy-Oriented Approach

In my view, a transition to strategy-oriented marketing is necessary to fulfill management's future expectations of the marketing function and its managers. The elements of strategy-oriented marketing and traditional marketing differ more in substance than in description. For example: Environmental scanning becomes environmental analysis, which requires the careful research of each major trend in our society, including its cross-impacts with other major trends, and the examination of the forces behind these trends. The purpose of this research and analysis is to identify interacting courses of events that have the potential for significant future impact on the business, and to generate related assumptions and issues.

Analysis of the cross-impacts of inflation and other major trends, and an examination of the underlying forces, might identify less obvious trends which generate an assumption and a separate issue related to inflation—with respect to consumers, customers and competitors. For example:

CONSUMER—
- *Assumption*—In an inflationary environment, consumers increasingly seek quality products that promise low maintenance and repair costs.
- *Issue*—Consumer purchases show an increasing preference for "experiences" over "things." Will inflation accelerate this trend and alter the future demand curve for consumer products?

CUSTOMER—
- *Assumption*—Inflation is accelerating retail concentration and increasing the purchasing leverage of the buyer.
- *Issue*—Inflation is changing consumer buying patterns. How will this change the retail distribution structure in the future?

COMPETITORS—
- *Assumption*—As inflation diminishes the international value of the dollar, imports from off-shore will increase and U.S. exports will decline.
- *Issue*—U.S. productivity is declining as inflation inhibits replacement of aging equipment. Will foreign producers expand U.S. manufacturing bases with more productive and advanced process technology?

As indicated by these illustrations, an analytical examination of even a generally corrosive trend like inflation can generate potentially useful assumptions—for example, the increased demand for high-quality products—in addition to key issues that must be considered in developing marketing plans.

In a traditional approach to consumer segmentation, surface demographics can identify an aging population, eroding growth rates in real disposable income and household formations, and a rather pessimistic outlook for the consumer market. Strategy-oriented segmentation requires analysis of the components of surface segments to identify leveragable trends. And, in fact, behind the surface population and income data in our illustration are some less obvious, more important, and highly leveragable trends. Consider:

- The greatest population bulge in American history has been moving into the prime working and consumer buying-age segment of 25 to 44 year-olds. The postwar baby boom—65 million youngsters born between World War II and the 1960 peak—will account for an unprecedented incease in the 25 to 44 age group by 1990.
- And, due in part to other interacting trends, including those relating to education and multiple incomes, these 25 to 44 year-olds will be unusually affluent. Their purchasing power is rising, with their expenditures anticipated to represent almost half of all consumer spending in 1985.

To this affluent bubble we should add the dramatic increase in working wives inside and outside of it, so that we can assume that the ability of consumers in general to buy will be high, despite inflation and the slowing growth in real disposable income.

But what will they buy? Through environmental analysis comes indication, as mentioned, of an increasing preference for "experiences" over "things." Strategy-oriented segmentation delves further into consumer motivation or attitudinal segmentation—or what makes Emily tick? In this example, one of many variables would be life-styles, and one among many identifiable life-style trends is that toward personal fulfillment, a leveragable trend in the "experience" vs. "things" issues.

Personal- or self-fulfillment, of course, is not a new value system. It has been with us since the elusive search began back in the 1960's for the "real me," along with all of its attendant counterculture manifestations. But the value system has changed dramatically over two decades, and the value mainstream today is a blend of the work ethic of the 1950's with the self-fulfillment and self-expression ethics of the 1960's and early 1970's. This new direction says: "I will wring every experience out of life—not necessarily through achievement—but by doing everything there is to be done. But I need time and money to do it."

Time Budgeting Implications

We have already assumed that the affluent and the working-wife households will have money. But time is the variable that deserves the attention of the strategy-oriented marketer: time for "experiences," time for self-expression, time for working wives to handle two jobs. Time may become the most precious commodity of this decade, and time budgeting one of the most leveragable marketing variables.

Time budgeting includes the application of time to self-fulfilling "experiences," which augurs well for businesses involved in travel, adventure, hobbies, sports and entertainment. And time budgeting also includes the conservation of time in less fulfilling but necessary rituals—cooking, cleaning, shopping, getting things repaired, paying bills, and so on, ad infinitum. This promises to accelerate the growth of convenience products and services. So, this is where our strategy-oriented consumer segmentation leads us: Consumers will not be buying fewer things. Rather, they will be buying more convenient, time-conserving versions of "things," such as:

- Microwave cooking products, which save time, reduce work drudgery, and, as a bonus, save energy.
- Home computers, which will conserve time and energy in shopping, communicating, paying bills, and a host of other tasks.
- Video cassette recorders, which permit program selection and viewing at a time convenient to the owner.
- And also convenient services for the things they buy. With so many households empty during normal working hours—because of the growing number of one-person and two-worker households—marketers are changing their offerings to meet the consumers' time-budget problem. In a growing number of markets, for example, General Electric is providing service for large consumer durables products in the evening and on Saturday.

In short, behind the obvious and debilitating trend of inflation, and the obvious and pessimistic surface demographics, there are interactive segments in the environment and the consumer market which combine to present significant marketing opportunities—opportunities that would probably lie fallow for businesses using a traditional marketing approach.

Changes in Segmentation and Competitive Monitoring

My own company's experience confirms the benefits of strategy-oriented analysis in segmenting the customer market and in understanding the competitive situation. For one thing, in our kind of business—where our direct customers are resellers—storefront classifications are an outmoded method for segmenting retail customers. Analysis and examination on the basis of customer needs and methods of operation provide more meaningful trends. The objective in each segment identified is to provide a level of service that will minimize dealers' inventory requirements and conserve their working capital.

The final element of the traditional marketing process, and the next-to-last element in strategy-oriented marketing, is competitive analysis. Intensifying world competition, escalating technological responses to social and economic needs, and rampant inflation will be changing the competitive game—and also many of the players—in years to come. Traditional competitive analysis, however, only indicates where a competitor has been. It is increasingly important to know where key competitors plan to go, and where you can go and they cannot follow.

Value analysis of the material and labor content of their products, and a pro forma analysis of their financial structures and operating results, can provide insights into competitors' strengths and vulnerabilities, as well as an appreciation of the potential impacts of environmental changes on their future decisions. There is considerable financial information available in the public domain with respect to publicly held companies. This includes security analysts' reports, quarterly and annual reports of the Securities and Exchange Commission, local newspapers in competitors' plant cities, and many others. It requires creative financial analysis to mold an image of a competitor's anatomy, but it can be done, even for a conglomerate.

The benefits of creative, multifunctional competitive analysis are tangible. Understanding where the competition is going, and what its strengths and limitations are, can change a marketing operation from defensive to proactive—from catch up to one-upsmanship. It is a key element in the strategy-oriented marketing effort.

Contingency Planning

The strategy-oriented process has one additional element not present in traditional marketing, and that is contingency planning. In developing marketing plans founded on assumptions regarding future trends, it is important to have an escape hatch if one or more key variables start to veer off course.

A sensitivity analysis of key variables and the development of "What if . . ." scenarios with trigger points and action plans will help to maintain a strategic compass heading and to elevate the comfort level of management.

Strategy Base Is Essential

Clearly, I am a devotee of the strategy-oriented marketing effort. Any other approach to the future, in my view, could result in aimless wandering down unproductive side roads and blind alleys, in inverted priorities, in a misuse of marketing resources, and in a denial of future resources. To meet consumer and customer needs, to outflank competition, to leverage the competences of the business, and to meet management's expectations, the marketing plan for the future must have the appropriate strategic ingredients up front:

- The right kind of analysis—creative and in-depth;
- The right "What if . . ." questions; and
- The right priorities.

The marketing function continues its transition from an art form toward a management science. The transition represents a major contribution to business. But marketing people provide another important input to managerial judgment that must not be lost in the transition. That input is knowledge that is almost intuitive of the nuances of the marketplace—a knowledge that cannot be reduced to a quantifiable state and analyzed—plus an understanding of the real people who comprise the segments and how they might react to change. These strong visceral impulses are based on experience and learned perceptions, and they are the ground on which the marketing structure is built.

An anonymous Greek philosopher must have had strategy-oriented marketing people in mind when he wrote, "Fix your eyes on the stars, but beware of the potholes in the ground lest you stumble on the road to destiny."

The Broader Determinants of Market Strategy

George M. Zapp
Vice President—Planning and Development
Chemicals Group
PPG Industries, Inc.

MARKET STRATEGY is frequently shaped by the short-term urgency to achieve the volume and price required by the annual profit plan. For market strategy to be most productive, however, it must also be shaped by the long-range mission, objectives and strategy of the total enterprise. Market strategy can best fulfill its vital role by utilizing unique skills to achieve both the strategic objectives and the tactical plans of the total business.

The shorter range tactics, plans and programs for stimulating the productivity, effectiveness and motivation of the marketing function are all vital parts of the business planning effort. They are a derivative, however, of a broader strategy. Obviously, if short-term profit objectives are not achieved consistently, you do not have to worry too much about long-range strategy. But long-range profitability goes to those who manage their future, instead of reacting to current events.

Leaders within the marketing function can be more effective if they are conversant with basic strategic planning concepts. In providing an overview of some of the more important concepts, I propose to relate them to appropriate implementation strategy within the marketing discipline.

Some Strategic Concepts

The past two decades have witnessed the evolution of a number of new strategic planning methodologies. Four strategic concepts will be illustrated here. However, the essential criterion for strategic management is not so much the particular methodology chosen as it is the use of a strategic thinking process by managers as they operate their businesses.

The four concepts are:

(1) The strategic planning grid—as developed initially for "portfolio analyses" by the General Electric Company;

(2) The product life-cycle planning system—as developed, for example, by Arthur D. Little, Inc.;

(3) The experience curve theory—as developed for planning purposes by the Boston Consulting Group; and

(4) The PIMS (Profit Impact of Market Strategy) relationships—as developed by the Strategic Planning Institute.

Each of these concepts has the possibility of offering valuable insight into the strategic realities of the total enterprise and then into appropriate market strategy. There are, of course, alternatives and variants for each. Also, while each has its limitations as well as its merits, only an overview of their potential utility is presented here.

Exhibit 1: Strategic Planning Grid

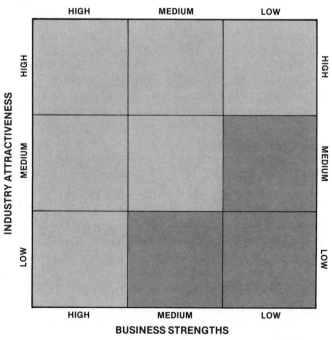

Source: PPG adaptation of General Electric Strategic Decision Matrix

Exhibit 2: Competitor Comparison

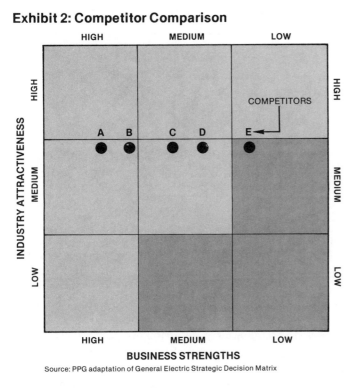

Source: PPG adaptation of General Electric Strategic Decision Matrix

Exhibit 3: Long-Range Plan

Current Year — Base Plan
X Ten Years from Now ...... Alternate

Source: PPG adaptation of General Electric Strategic Decision Matrix

Strategic Planning Grid

A demanding exercise for expansion-minded market strategists is the use of the strategic planning grid to assess the strategic strengths and weaknesses of the business in comparison with the competition and in comparison to other businesses. The results can be pictorially represented on a strategic planning grid, such as the one shown in Exhibit 1.

The horizontal axis provides a measure of a product line's business strength in comparison to competitors. The vertical axis measures the relative attractiveness of the industry in which the product line is competing.

Businesses that are located in the lower right hand corner of this grid are candidates for harvesting or divestiture. Businesses in the upper left-hand corner are candidates for aggressive funding for growth. Businesses located in the diagonal area from lower left to upper right require attention and ingenuity to move them out of there and into the upper left corner. Failure to achieve this objective usually results in the business gradually sinking into the lower right area, with the resulting undesirable fate.

It is a good discipline to determine the position on the grid of both your product and those of your principal competitors, so as to test the reality of your proposed market strategy. (See Exhibit 2.) Obviously, if you are Company E on the grid of Exhibit 2, and your marketing thrust calls for you to become an aggressive industry leader, it could turn out to be a valiant, but kamikaze charge unless there is some major strategic innovation in your business that permits such a radical restructuring of the industry.

There are instances of a new competitor in an industry leapfrogging competition to become a leader. For example, Halcon (Oxirane) developed an innovative, low-cost process for manufacturing the chemical commodity, propylene glycol, a business that the company was not in at the time. Its entry with this innovation forced essentially everyone—except the leader, Dow—out of the U.S. manufacture of this product.

Generally, it requires a significant strategic innovation to achieve a major restructuring of market share. Planning for such a restructuring through marketing strategy alone is frequently a costly, low-percentage option. What usually happens over the time span of a long-range plan is that consolidation occurs as the industry matures and the weaker factors exit, as illustrated in Exhibit 3. The leader must be careful during this period not to harvest its market share prematurely.

Life-Cycle Strategic Analysis

Another potentially useful strategic discipline for analyzing a business and determining appropriate business and functional strategies is the life-cycle planning system as developed, for example, by Arthur D. Little, Inc.

This discipline divides the life span of each business or product into four distinct segments. Each segment has its own strategic characteristics and each should be managed with a different business and marketing strategy. The segments are the well-known "Embryonic," "Growth," "Mature" and "Aging."

Exhibit 4: Life Cycles for Commodity Chemicals

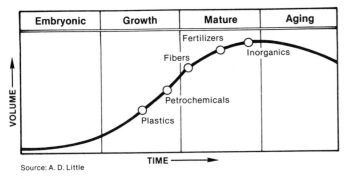

Source: A. D. Little

Exhibit 5: Continuous Renewal over Life Cycle

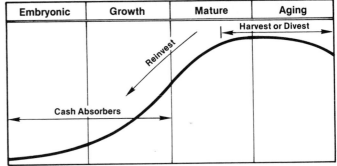

Source: A. D. Little

The life-cycle concept can be used to categorize general classes of businesses, such as "specialty chemicals" vs. "commodity chemicals," in order to facilitate analysis of their different life-cycle characteristics. Or the products within a class of chemicals can be located on the life cycle and appropriate strategy developed for each (Exhibit 4).

An important part of the life-cycle discipline is the strategic management of cash flow and the appropriate assignment of functional management in each of the segments. Exhibit 5 depicts the management of cash flow by harvesting businesses in the "Late Mature" and "Aging" segments, and utilizing the strengths of the research and marketing functions to reinvest that cash flow into cash-absorbing new "Embryonic" and "Growth" products. The business thereby continues to regenerate itself. An excellent example of a company applying this is DuPont, which recently announced that is was phasing out of the mature dyestuffs business. At about the same time, it also announced several new products and expansions.

Organizational and managerial strategy also require different types of human resources and functional disciplines for the different segments of the life cycle. For example, the general management emphasis needs to shift from "entrepreneurial" to "marketer" to "administrator" to "milker" as the business passes through its life cycle (Exhibit 6). Similarly, marketing strategy needs to focus on the market research and commercial

development disciplines when the business is in its embryonic stage. The emphasis gradually changes to a traditional marketing mix and then to tough competitive selling as the product's aging phase is approached.

An important application of this concept is the comparison of the portfolio of products or businesses of your company with those of your competitors. In Exhibit 7, Company B may have a higher return on investment and a better looking balance sheet than Company A, but it may be heading for serious trouble because it has fallen into the "mature business trap." By following a business and market strategy of continued strengthening and reinvesting in its already strong but mature businesses, management has failed to utilize the strengths of the company's marketing and research functions and the cash flow from its mature businesses to regenerate the total enterprise with new products. Company A, on the other hand, has managed the regeneration process in an ideal manner.

The Experience Curve and Marketing Strategy

An intriguing strategic concept, from a market strategy viewpoint, is the "experience curve." The Boston Consulting Group has determined that in most cases, with value-added products, the unit cost of manufacture, in constant dollars, declines about 20 to 30 percent every time the cumulative production volume doubles. On a

Exhibit 6: Managerial Strategy in Life-Cycle Stages

Embryonic	Growth	Mature	Aging
	General Management Focus		
Entrepreneur	Marketer	Administrator	Milker
	Marketing Focus		
Market Research, Commercial Development	Market Strategy, Application Development	Sales	Lean and Mean

Source: A. D. Little

Exhibit 7: Competitive Portfolio Analysis

Embryonic	Growth	Mature	Aging

Company A

Company B

Source: A. D. Little

Exhibit 8: Relationship of Cost and Experience

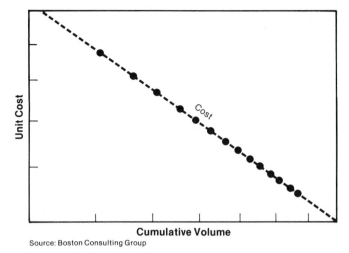

Source: Boston Consulting Group

Exhibit 9: Stable Price Pattern with Increased Volume

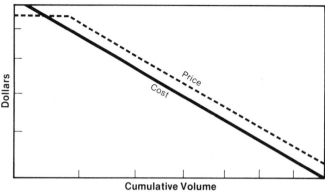

Source: Boston Consulting Group

log-log graph, this relationship yields the straight line indicated in Exhibit 8.

If two competitors maintain the same market share and have comparable production histories, they should have comparable manufacturing costs (so long as they both started out at the same time, grew at the same rate, and maintained similar market shares). As soon as one of them gains market share consistently, however, that firm's costs start declining much more rapidly than the other producer's. (A later example shows how a strong marketing strategy can be built upon this market share/product cost relationship.)

In general, price on a constant-dollar basis in a stable competitive market should also decline as the cost of the industry leader declines (Exhibit 9), provided the cost/price relationship of the leading producer stays constant during the period (a possibility if the leader is also the price-setter in the market, which isn't necessarily the case). Under these circumstances, the leader is left with a comfortable margin, while the industry laggards keep struggling. An unstable price situation develops when price does not decline in concert with cost. Competition is

quickly attracted by inflated margins and price pressures suddenly dissipate profit margins (Exhibit 10).

A dynamic strategy for an innovative company with confidence in its technology and marketing resources is outlined in Exhibit 11. Here the industry leader introduces a new product and prices it at a level consistent with a volume it anticipates achieving in the future. If the product has the planned price elasticity, the targeted volume usually follows.

By following this strategy on a continuous basis, an innovator can literally drive down the experience curve, buying market share at the earlier stages of product introduction when it costs less to buy. At an appropriate point in time—when market share dominance and lowest production costs are clearly established—prices can be allowed to revert to a pricing level that will provide a handsome return to the innovator, but permit the lagging producers just to stay in business.

Probably the best publicized practitioner of the experience curve strategy has been Texas Instruments. The company's innovative technology base, plus its finely tuned strategic planning system, has given management the confidence to drive relentlessly down the experience curve to establish a powerful market share and cost position as compared with both the U.S. and the Japanese semiconductor industry.

Exhibit 10: Unstable Price Pattern with Increased Volume

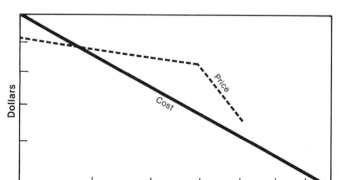

Source: Boston Consulting Group

Exhibit 11: Market Share Pricing Strategy

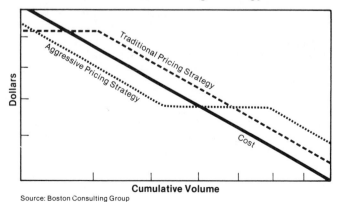

Source: Boston Consulting Group

Much has been published recently about the "decline" of the experience curve and the "decline" in the relationship between market share and profitability. Some of this may be belated recognition that, under certain circumstances, creative strategic options can be developed to protect a business from the impact of macro strategic forces. A small producer developing a protected market niche is just one example. These are issues beyond the scope of this overview presentation.

PIMS—"Profit Impact of Market Strategy"

The Strategic Planning Institute has developed a number of very meaningful strategic correlations as a result of examining data from over 1,500 businesses. The Institute has identified at least nine different variables that have a significant strategic influence upon the performance of a business:

(1) Investment intensity;
(2) Productivity;
(3) Market position;
(4) Market growth;
(5) Quality;
(6) Innovation and/or differentiation;
(7) Vertical integration;
(8) Cost escalation;
(9) Current strategic effort.

The first six of these variables are particularly important in any business and market strategy for an industrial product line. Two of these—investment intensity and market position—serve to illustrate the usefulness of this discipline in developing a market strategy.

Capital Intensity vs. Profitability

For the broad spectrum of businesses studied, the PIMS data indicate that there is an inverse relationship between the capital intensity of a business and its profitability—that is, the higher the capital intensity, the poorer the return on investment. (See Exhibit 12.)

If you have the good fortune already to be in a business with relatively low capital intensity, there are certain effective and ineffective market strategies that one should emphasize or avoid. Among the more effective market strategies to optimize profitability of a low capital-intensity business are:

(1) Maintaining a high market share in the total market.
(2) Concentrating market share so as to be a major factor in the important market segments, instead of dissipating strength across all market segments.
(3) Being a leader in the strategically important market segments.

Exhibit 12: PIMS Data on Capital Intensity vs. Profitability

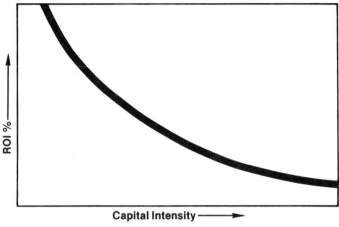

Source: Strategic Planning Institute

(4) If product differentiation possibilities exist, making sure you are a leader in the strategically important ones.
(5) Maintaining high quality.
(6) Maintaining a strong marketing effort.

There are also some relatively ineffective strategies, for a low capital-intensive business, among which are the following:

(1) Spending investment capital on backward integration.
(2) Maintaining high inventories.
(3) Dedicating scarce resources to aggressive cost reduction rather than to strong marketing and product differentiation.

Exhibit 13: PIMS Data on Market Share vs. Profitability

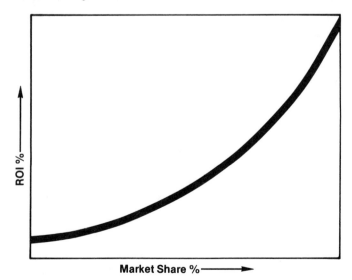

Source: Strategic Planning Institute

Market Share vs. Profitability

The PIMS studies have also confirmed a direct relationship between market share and profitability (Exhibit 13). If a company is blessed with a moderately high market share on a product line, there are certain market strategies that appear generally to be either effective or ineffective if the firm wants to maintain and optimize that position.

Among the more effective market strategies for a high market share business are these:

(1) Protect market share until the life-cycle maturity or other strategic factors indicate that it is more profitable to harvest the share.

(2) Maintain a strong marketing program.

(3) Maintain a high research effort so as to continue the innovative image of the product line.

(4) Pace the introduction of new or differentiated products so as to balance the need for innovation and product line renewal with the financial burdens of too many new product introductions.

(5) Concentrate market strengths in the strategically important market segments.

(6) Maintain high product quality.

Among the more ineffective market strategies for a high market-share business are:

(1) Concentrate resources on cost reduction instead of marketing strategies.

(2) Balance the cash-flow requirements of the product line too early in its life cycle.

(3) Harvest market share prematurely.

Some Conclusions

The most effective market plan is one that is built upon a solid strategic foundation that is derived from the long-range strategic plan for the total enterprise and for the product line. Tactics and programs to enhance the effectiveness of market plans are absolutely essential. Unless they are built upon a solid strategic foundation, however, even inferior competition can effectively exploit a basic strategic business vulnerability, and undermine your position.

The overview of the strategic disciplines presented here by no means includes the only ones available. And, unfortunately, it is possible to give only limited illustrations here of their full utility and power. It should be noted, also, that these various approaches are not necessarily applicable for all product/market situations. The critical factor is not the choice of the planning system, but the choice to think and manage strategically.

A company's senior management needs to recognize, too, that the effectiveness of both strategic business planning and market planning can be enhanced by a close working partnership between these two functions. Each brings strengths and skills that are essential to an effective total business planning process.

Relevant Strategy Options and Priorities

John R. Rhode
Vice President—Marketing and Planning
Industrial Products Group
Combustion Engineering, Inc.

THE LEVELS OF PLANNING within a company may be likened to a pyramid, with the overall corporate objectives as the apex and the business-unit and product-line objectives, strategies and tactics resting at successively lower levels of the same structure. (See Exhibit 1.) This is an apt metaphor since the blocks that make up each lower level of the pyramid need not be the same as those in the levels above; yet they must support and be compatible with the higher levels, or else the whole structure will collapse.

In most multimarket corporations, overall goals and objectives are set forth by the chief executive officer. These broad statements of mission, though reasonable and desirable for the corporation as a whole, are not necessarily appropriate in their entirety for guiding the direction of any individual business unit or product line. (For example, Combustion Engineering has 33 business units that market some 200 product lines, or serve what we call 200 product-market segments.)

Managing each individual product line in such a way as to meet every stated corporate-wide goal could very well require actions that would not be in the best interest of the company as a whole. In some cases, for example, it would result in the manager's emphasizing measures of performance that should not be the major focus of his operation. In others, it would result in a manager's being satisfied with levels of performance significantly below the operation's actual capability. And, in far too many cases, it would result in the manager's developing strategies and tactics having high risk and low probability of success, or else being overly optimistic in projections of performance.

If the product-line manager should not use the corporate objectives and goals as those for his or her own operation, then what should be used? The answer is to rely on an analysis of the line's external environment, markets, customers and competitors, thereby narrowing down the relevant options. Although there are many conceptual frameworks available for environmental analysis, some are inappropriate for this purpose because they deal with the problems of managing a mixed "portfolio" of multiple business units. They may also be too abstract or call for too many subjective judgments—and therefore are not suitable for use by the typical business-unit or product-line team.

Exhibit 1: Product-Line Support for Corporate Goals and Objectives

CORPORATE GOALS AND OBJECTIVES

BUSINESS-UNIT GOALS AND PRODUCT-LINE OBJECTIVES

PRODUCT-LINE STRATEGIES

PRODUCT-LINE TACTICS

Market Maturity Cycle: Potential Planning Tool

One analytical framework that has proved valuable in the product-line planning of business units within the Industrial Products Group of Combustion Engineering is the "maturity cycle." The maturity cycle concept can be applied to a business, a product line, an individual product, or even a homogeneous group of customers. It has its greatest validity and inevitability in those situations where technological substitution takes place over time in your products or markets (or in your customers' products or markets).

For purposes of discussion, the practical application of such concepts in my own company will be used to illustrate the analysis of strategy options and priorities within a single, identifiable market—usually that for a single product line. According to this version of the life-cycle concept as we employ it, most markets go through three distinct phases during their evolution: growth, maturity and decline. It is sometimes helpful to break the growth phase further into early-growth and late-growth stages (Exhibit 2).

During the early-growth phase of the cycle, the market is normally served by a single pioneer company or, at most, two or three suppliers (Exhibit 3). The high, accelerating growth rates during this phase are due to mounting awareness of the ability of this particular product or service to fulfill a previously unfilled need—or to do it better than whatever it replaces.

As the market enters the later stages of the growth phase, more competitors are normally drawn to the field by the promising high growth rate. But this rate, while remaining high, will have stopped increasing and will actually begin to decrease as the market approaches transition to the mature stage. Until now, supply has been in rough balance with demand, or possibly lagging it. During transition to the mature market, supply will normally outpace demand, and the market will enter a period of at least temporary surplus capacity. Heightened competitive pressures characteristic of this transition stage may lead to a competitive shakeout and a reduction of margins for the remaining competitors.

The maturity phase of the market is characterized by relatively modest growth rates and a fairly stable competitive and pricing structure. The final declining phase of the market cycle usually comes when a product or service becomes the victim of substitution of a newer product or newer technology. (In some instances, the pattern for industrial products actually reflects substitutions being made for customers' products or services.) The declining phase is also normally one of declining margins and competitive exits.

There are, of course, several variations to the "normal" market evolution. Sometimes external factors cause a market to enter a second growth phase or, possibly, a premature decline. Rapid changes in the supply and cost of energy during the 1970's, for example, altered the traditional evolution of many markets.

Exhibit 2: Characteristics of Maturity-Cycle Phases

EARLY GROWTH
- one or only a few competitors
- high and rising growth rates
- substitution effect

LATE GROWTH
- competitive entry
- high but declining growth rates
- substitution saturation

TRANSITION
- surplus capacity
- competitive pressures and shakeout
- reduced margins

MATURITY
- lower growth rates
- stable competitive and pricing structure

DECLINE
- substitution victim
- reduced margins
- competitive exits

Product-Line Implications

To the extent that market phases determine product-line strategies, there are three basic areas of emphasis for product-line management. They are growth, profits and cash flow. All priorities and objectives established with respect to these should agree with the position of the product-line's market in the maturity cycle.

Exhibit 3: Preferred Product-Line Strategies and Tactics, Early Growth Market Phase

- Emphasis in goals and objectives
  Growth

- Strategy
  Growth through market expansion of primary demand

- Tactics
  Advertising . . . . High, aimed at product awareness
  R and D . . . . High, kept technologically current
  Price . . . . Two options:
    • based on customer value
    • based on production cost
  Commitment. . . High level of resources kept available over extended period for primary market development

If the seller's product line has a pioneer role in the early growth stage of the market, then the major emphasis must be on growth. Attempts to emphasize either profits or cash flow at this stage would almost certainly doom the line to failure. Strategy for growth, which can be achieved either through market expansion or market penetration, in this case should concentrate on market expansion through developing primary demand. The seller's major investments, therefore, should be in establishing a customer base and the required channels of distribution to bring the product to market.

Advertising should aim at stimulating primary demand, and R and D outlays should be relatively high to assure that the line stays abreast of any changing technology. (In the company where senior management is disposed to an early fixation on profits or return on investment, it might be advantageous—for internal management purposes, at least—to capitalize some of the expenses going into the establishment of an early market position. For example, the customers a business generates early in its life are going to be longer term assets than the brick and mortar that the accounting profession allows us to capitalize and amortize over the life of the business.)

There are two options available in pricing the line. The most frequently employed in the growth stage is what might be called "skimming." In exercising this option, unit prices are set at a relatively high level, but slightly lower than the value the customer derives using this product as replacement for the one previously used. The second option is to price on the basis of the present or future cost of producing the product.

A low price may have the effect of increasing the growth of primary demand and of delaying the entrance of at least some potential competitors. This option should be considered only if there is strong commitment from management to provide the resources necessary to expand capacity to meet demand, despite somewhat lower profits at the outset. It would make no sense at all, of course, to keep prices low and stimulate a demand that the seller would be unable or unwilling to satisfy. Such a shortfall would probably draw at least as many competitors as the skimming price option.

Under either pricing option, management should not underestimate the amount of time or resources normally required to make a financial success out of a pioneering business unit. Research by the Strategic Planning Institute indicates that, on average, a "start-up" business will require six years to break even.[1] And many of the business units whose experiences were reflected in SPI's "start-up" data base were not actual pioneers in their markets.

This issue of commitment cannot be overemphasized. In one situation, a company entered a new market area with a new production facility. The company's financial projections indicated profitable operations by the end of the second year and an attractive return on investment early in the fourth year. The business unit selling the line, while making steady progress in the marketplace, was not meeting its projections. As pressure built, the unit began proliferating products and applications in the line in a vain attempt to live up to its advance billing. This dispersion of the unit's resources slowed its progress in its major market area, and now that unit's manufacturing facility is being used as an "R and D" facility. The previous management team has either left the company or disappeared into the corporate structure. Such a situation, unfortunately, is all too common when management fails to recognize the commitment required to make any market entry successful.

The Late-Growth Phase

If the market for a product line is in the later stages of its growth phase, there may be an opportunity to balance growth with profitability. For example, if the line was a pioneer entry in the market, a good deal of the investment in establishing its customer base and distribution channels may now be behind it.

In the face of newly arrived competition, many aspects of the pioneer's previous tactics should change. (See Exhibit 4.) Advertising, for example, should focus on particular features of the product, and the building of product differentiation should become a major goal of both advertising and R and D programs. If the seller was a market pioneer, with a strong market position already established, it should be able to shift its major investment thrust toward facilities needed to continue to grow at or near the market rate. Marketing research should now be aimed at identifying significant customer segments and intensifying attention to the differentiated needs of those segments. R and D should aim at product refinement, with focus again on those segments of the total market selected for major concentration. Pricing in the market at this point will become soft as the effect of excess supply increases competitive pressures. As the end of this phase approaches, it is important for the line's management to become more cautious in adding facilities to meet increased demand. Wherever possible, such additions should be made in relatively small increments, utilizing general-purpose equipment.

If the business unit selling the line was a follower in the market, then in the market's late-stage growth phase, its own emphasis will also need to be on growth—both from expansion of the basic market and from market penetration. While many of its required tactics are the same as for the market pioneer at this stage in the life cycle, the follower will simultaneously be investing in the development of its customer base and distribution channels, as well as in facilities to meet market demand.

---

[1] *The Start-Up Business Report.* Strategic Planning Institute, 1978.

Exhibit 4: Preferred Product-Line Strategies and Tactics, Late Growth Market Phase

```
• Emphasis in goals and objectives
    Pioneer:
        Growth balanced with profits
    Follower:
        Growth

• Strategy
    Pioneer:
        Maintain position and market share
    Follower:
        Growth through market penetration

• Tactics
    Pioneer:
        Advertising and
            R and D . . . . . Product differentiation and
                             refinement
        Production . . . . Small increments balancing
                             with demand
        Marketing . . . . . Marget segmentation
    Follower:
        Commitment. . . Investment
                           • customer base
                           • distribution
                           • facilities
        Marketing . . . . . Penetrate before maturity
```

It is very important during this period for the seller to try to judge the length of time remaining before the market makes the transition into its maturity stage. But this is especially crucial for the follower, since the strategies and tactics employed to penetrate the market are chosen so that most of the penetration will have been accomplished before the transition occurs. Increased competitive pressures and lower growth rates in the market will soon make further market penetration much more costly and more likely to draw strong competitive reaction.

The Maturity Phase

An understanding of the substitution effect largely responsible for the initial rapid growth of the market enables planners to estimate the timing of the end of the growth phase. Customers may increasingly substitute a generic product offering for that of a specialized product traditionally used before, or industrial product users may increasingly substitute products of their own manufacture for certain products traditionally purchased from outside suppliers.

As the product-line's market reaches maturity, the seller's goals must put greater emphasis on profits than on growth, with profits being measured primarily by return on net assets. In this phase, strategies should con-

centrate on developing differential advantages for specific market segments. Differential advantage can be defined as a value that is sought by a significant group of customers, for which they are willing to pay a premium, and which they believe can be uniquely supplied by a particular supplier. If such a differential advantage cannot be created, the product tends toward commodity status, to be sold primarily on the basis of price.

Just to reinforce this point: There are only two reasons why a customer will buy a product from one seller instead of another. Perceiving no other differential between the sellers' product offerings, the customer will buy the one with the lower price. Alternatively, the customer will choose the other product offering—and be willing to pay a premium for it—if it promises what are judged to be extra advantages. Beyond the production of the product itself, a manufacturer provides a great deal more—including warranty backup, product service, credit policies, inventory policies, assistance from a trained sales force, channel of distribution, physical distribution, reseller support, advertising and other promotional support—all of which are actually part of the product offering.

It is not necessary for the seller to capitalize on a net differential advantage it has by charging a higher price, although this is not uncommon. The seller may decide instead to convert the benefits of that differential advantage into an increased market share. Thus, given the market-phase positions of some of our business units, there are situations where I advise them to maintain relative price parity with their competitors in the marketplace because it appears that the long-term goals of their units (and the long-term benefits to the company as a whole) would be maximized by their holding an increased market share rather than by generating increased profits.

During the maturity stage, the R and D support that exists should emphasize value engineering—that is, achieving the lowest possible cost without sacrificing quality. (See Exhibit 5.) The product offering may be pruned to meet the changing and somewhat reduced customer needs. Marketing research should aim at identifying the specific market segments that are most promising and rely to the greatest extent possible on publicly available information. Management may even want to consider subcontracting certain of its manufacturing steps in order to avoid large incremental additions in capacity. If this tactic is adopted, however, the seller's business unit must still maintain control of the marketing activity.

The Capital-Intensive Business

Sound strategy is absolutely essential for those struggling with a highly capital-intensive business. It is easy to wallow around in a tough competitive situation without

Exhibit 5: Preferred Product-Line Strategies and Tactics, Maturity Market Phase

```
• Emphasis in goals and objectives
     Profits balanced with growth

• Strategy
     Hold position
     Concentrate on specific market segments

• Tactics
     Marketing . . . . . Focus resources
                        Prune line
                        Identify prime segments
                        Promote differential
                             advantages
                        Price competitively
     Production and
        R and D . . . . . Lowest cost
                        • value engineering
                        • expand cautiously
                        • consider subcontracting
```

really establishing any clear direction and without coming to any clear-cut decision on whether to stay in the market or to get out.

An example is a former business which relied on a very old plant. This business was not as capital intensive as many other businesses, because a lot of the investment had been amortized. But in order to fully utilize that old plant, we had added a number of products to the line that used the same manufacturing technology as the main products. In all of these add-on areas, however, the business was a marginal latecomer in a mature market, and never established a strong competitive position. The mix of products was maintained with the rationale that this increased the capacity utilization. (As everybody knows, and accountants always remind us, when you have a lot of unabsorbed overhead it helps to spread it around and think in terms of contribution pricing, contribution margins, and the like.)

A serious study of the situation finally concluded that the only solution to this business's profit problems in a mature market was to increase market share. Yet there was no real way of increasing market share by increasing sales without instigating disastrous price competition. For this reason, another approach was chosen to increasing market share—that of decreasing sales. This may sound unusual, but if you can decrease your sales proportionately less than you decrease your market size, the arithmetic for computing this basic ratio ensures that your market share is going to go up.

Over the strong objections of many of the manufacturing and accounting people in the business, a lot of products were cut from the line. Miscellaneous items were pruned away that had been added to the line, forcing everything back to the basic product offering which had a

good reputation and a very strong market position. Interestingly enough, that particular business has since generated its highest profits—its highest return on investment—in a history that goes back to 1850. Unfortunately, as the accountants continue to remind us, its capacity utilization is still not up to that of some of our other businesses. Nevertheless, by facing up to the strategy issue, and by concentrating our resources and strengths in areas where we really had a significant competitive advantage, we were able to increase our profit return significantly.

Misplaced Growth Emphasis

The most common error made during the maturity phase of the market cycle is to emphasize growth through penetration. In one case, the management of a distribution business serving a mature, low-growth market decided to emphasize growth as one objective. Early efforts in this direction were extremely successful, and in a period of less than five years actual sales were increased tenfold. Even when the results are corrected for an increase in prices, management was spectacularly successful in meeting its stated goal of increased growth through market penetration.

Unfortunately, near the end of this period, established competitors began to react "irrationally." Management had accomplished its dramatic increase in penetration, not by price concessions, but by offering products and services tailored to the needs of the customers. After a while, competitors were no longer able to ignore their resulting market-share and volume losses. Since most were family-owned, single-market businesses, they chose to remain and fight in the marketplace rather than to liquidate. The net effect was to ensure severely reduced prices and margins in this market. As a result, no major competitor in this market was able to obtain an acceptable level of profit.

The fact is that the "survival instinct" behavior of competitors was entirely predictable when the initial management action is viewed in the context of the prevailing maturity cycle. At least two mistakes were made by management of the business. One was an overemphasis on growth as the primary objective for the business, given its mature market. The second was the degree to which the growth achieved came from rapid penetration of the market. If growth had indeed been necessary to provide desired financial returns for this particular business, it should have been developed at a slower rate and at least part of it should have come from a geographical expansion of the market rather than from increased penetration.

As Your Competitor Sees It

There is also another lesson in this experience for product-line management. It is wise to consider what the market and your marketing actions look like from the standpoint of your competitor. I am especially reminded of this on those occasions when business-unit or product-line managers come to me and say, it is really incredible, but XYZ Company must have completely lost its senses. The culprits in such cases are often described as acting totally irrationally and irresponsibly—or, in a favorite euphemism, as being "bad competitors." What this usually means is that they push the price button too frequently, and lower their prices.

But it is my impression that, in most cases, no competitors act irrationally—certainly not as they see the situation. When a management team says that there is an irrational competitor in its market, my first suspicion is that insufficient efforts have been made to analyze the competitor's position. We have found it useful to have someone from our headquarters planning staff help in organizing a session to make such a competitive analysis. For this purpose, we may bring together marketing people, sales people and anyone else who may have information on the competitor in question. We assemble in a room with a blackboard and a flip-chart, and spend as much time as necessary to analyze all the relevant information we can on that competitor. In time, we can begin to see the competitive market situation through that competitor's eyes, rather than through our own.

For example, in the case of the distribution business mentioned earlier, I recall some of our people coming into the competitive review session talking about these bad actors who were cutting price and causing chaos in the market, whereas they themselves had been statesmanlike and maintained their price levels. But by the time the session was over, they realized that they had really triggered the price competition by the approach that they had taken to the market.

If you encounter a competitor who doesn't appear to be playing the game according to the logic of the market phase, perhaps the situation is being seen in a different light. There are times, of course, when a competitor actually does intend, for whatever reason, to destabilize the market. At that point, even if you have a leading position, you have very basic decisions to make.

One approach is to try and do nothing, an approach that normally occurs to our management teams. They think, if we ignore the competitor, it will stop doing those stupid things and go away; and in time, it will see the error of its ways and raise prices again. Unfortunately, there are many cases, especially when the market is in a mature or declining stage, where the competitor's price competition is going to be very successful. It will result in a larger market share, which will further encourage it to continue its price competition. Then, belatedly, we may decide to match its prices and have problems living with the resulting low margins.

My view is that you simply have to decide, when this kind of competition first occurs, whether or not the market is one that you are willing to defend. If you are willing to do so because you believe the market to be a long way from its declining stage, or because you believe that it uniquely fits or supports other products in your portfolio which you do not want to lose, then I think you have to meet the competition in battle. In some cases, you may even beat them, by cutting prices even further yourself in an attempt to restabilize the market after a period of time. You may find that a competitor's price cutting was really a desperation move and part of the death throes of that company in that market.

On the other hand, if you decide that the market is not worth defending in the long run, then you may want to shift to a "harvest" strategy. In so doing, you may decide to maintain price; if so, make sure that you get something in exchange for the market share that you are giving away. By this, I mean that you might reduce the ancillary services you have been giving—or your R and D or marketing support. You could even reduce the quality of your product to some extent. Because of inertia accumulated from your prior position, especially when that has been a leading position in the market, it will take a while for your customers to really perceive what you have done to your product. Meanwhile, you will be trading off that position and still gaining from the money originally spent in developing your customer case during earlier phases of the market. The biggest mistake you can make is not recovering that money when you give up your asset.

The Market Decline Phase

Once a market reaches the end of its mature cycle and moves into decline, management should shift its emphasis toward cash flow. (See Exhibit 6.) There are, of course, two ways of developing cash flow from an established business. One, that of harvesting, tends to sell off the company's market position and customer base built up over years, by reducing the level of service or

Exhibit 6: Preferred Product-Line Strategies and Tactics, Declining Market Phase

- Emphasis in goals and objectives
  Cash flow

- Strategy
  Sell off market position—harvest; or divest or
  liquidate business unit

- Tactics
  Production . . . . Reduce service and quality
  Marketing . . . . . Maintain price
  R and D,
    Advertising
    and Market
    Research. . . . Minimize or eliminate

quality in the product while not providing a corresponding reduction in price. (During this period, expenses on R and D, advertising and marketing research are kept to a minimum, if any are made at all.)

The other method of increasing cash flow from a business is by divestment, either through liquidation or sale. In most cases, a harvest winds up in liquidation. It is sometimes possible, especially if the management team perceives a real substitution threat before it becomes generally recognized, to sell the business at a price that does not reflect the impending decline.

In any case, management of a product line must be careful in making the transition from emphasizing profits to emphasizing cash flow, since it is very difficult to reverse direction once the harvesting procedure has begun. When the decline in market position associated with a harvesting strategy begins, the downward momentum builds and the resources required to reverse that trend mount rapidly, especially in a mature or declining market.

Clearly, the different stages in the market life cycle for a business or product line call for somewhat different sets of skills to implement the required strategies properly. Many successful businesses have tended to concentrate their efforts on only certain segments of the cycle, preferring either to enter late or exit early with their product offerings via acquisition or divestiture, respectively. For instance, some corporations with finely honed skills as pioneers have been very successful at developing markets, and then selling off their positions or moving into new segments before the competitive turbulence associated with the late stages of the market's growth phase develops. Others have been successful in "quick-follower" roles, preferring to wait until a new market proves itself before they enter and attempt to out innovate the pioneer. Until recently, this was true of many Japanese firms.

Planning Dialogues with Senior Management

I have described potentially useful approaches in developing market strategy for a company's business units and product lines. What about the practical issue of how strategic thinking at this level can be kept compatible with the intentions of senior general management?

I do not believe that corporate strategy should be a straitjacket in which managers of individual business units and product lines must develop their objectives and goals. Each of these managers should first make an objective assessment of a line's external environments—the mix and range of the line, the competitors, the customer base, etc. After developing objectives and goals believed to be consistent with that external environment, the manager needs an early review of these in light of the *internal* company environment.

At my own company, some time ago we introduced the change in our planning process that is vital if product-line planning is to be truly effective. Previously, we had asked each business-unit and product-line manager to develop a strategic plan, complete with summaries of strategy and the tactical elements in the operating plan. All of these proposals were then submitted to general management. Too often, management would then say: "This is not good enough, you'll have to do better." The reaction might be: We have to have more profits, or greater growth, or better penetration in that particular market, or whatever.

The inevitable result was a last-minute effort to juggle the numbers. And that was easy. If that original figure was not good enough, then we will increase our gross margin by a half a percent; and, while we are at it, let us up the market share figure by 2 percent. It was all an exercise in using the calculator, and the result was two messages coming down clearly to the planners. One message said that the most important input in a strategic plan was to discover early what your boss considered acceptable. The second said that analyzing the market environment for a line was largely a meaningless ritual, since it was not going to amount to much at the critical approval point.

Under new planning procedures, once product-line planners have performed their environmental analyses, and suggested objectives and goals they believe to be consistent with the findings, general management has an opportunity at an early stage to review the proposals. If a senior manager decides that this is not what he had in mind for a particular line, he can say so early.

There are two differences in this approach. First, review time is scheduled much earlier, so there is more time for careful reevaluation. Second, a true dialogue can now take place. The product-line manager reports: This is the way we analyze our environment; our market, we believe, is in this stage; here are what we see as our competitive strengths and weaknesses and those of our competitors. The manager can also argue: You believe that we should be aggressive in this market. We see a declining market that calls for a quite different strategy. We need to reexamine the market to determine which view of the market is correct.

Unfortunately, top management often views product lines and units not in the context of their actual environment but, rather, as these businesses were when they used to run them—or as they would like them to be. That is a difficult situation to resolve. The early-stage dialogue just described, however, gives more support to the strategic analysis necessary to compete effectively in the marketplace.

In summary, (a) the relevant options and priorities for each product line are unique to that line and constrained by the external environment; (b) objectives, strategies and tactics formulated for a line must be consistent with each other and with the state of relative maturity of the market; and (c) an objective assessment of the risks and skill requirements associated with a particular course of action, plus a matching of these against the organization's needs and capabilities, must precede senior management's approval of plans proposed for a line.

Part II

Formulating Strategy for the Consumer Product Line

Identifying New Competitive Opportunities

David B. Smart
Director, Food Enterprises Division
Ralston Purina Company

THE A. C. NIELSEN COMPANY tracks new items that are introduced in grocery stores, as well as older items that are discontinued. The introduction of new items has been declining steadily since the mid-1970's. To quote Nielsen:[1] "There are probably several reasons involved, but an important one must be the closer scrutiny given new items. To a great extent the buying function has been mechanized, and buyers are equipped with up-to-the-minute factual data on product movement which often contradict the benign forecasts offered by salesmen."

Intense competitive pressures continue to rise, and what is true in the grocery store is true in all markets. For manufacturers generally, a key question is how to identify opportunities in a churning, volatile marketplace where both competitive pressures and the cost of remaining in the game are increasing at an unrelenting rate. A review of recent examples suggest that there are some areas that can be profitably explored for new competitive opportunities. These include:

(1) Media strategy
(2) Product positioning
(3) Product profile
(4) A new niche in the marketplace
(5) Product differences
(6) Distribution patterns
(7) Line extensions
(8) Opportunities in packaging
(9) Demographics

Media Strategy

It is possible for smaller dollars, if concentrated, to outperform bigger dollars. This was the case in a recent

[1] *The Nielsen Researcher*, No. 6, 1978.

situation, for example, where two manufacturers between them shared approximately 70 percent of the market for a commodity-like packaged food product. The category was slowly declining in response to long-term socioeconomic trends.

The leading brand maintained its share dominance with the support of a national advertising program—primarily on network television and in women's magazines. The second brand undertook an exhaustive and detailed analysis of sales by geographic and demographic segments. Its media dollars were then shifted into spot TV, ethnic media, and bus transport cards. Although outspent totally in media dollar support, the second brand was able to arrest the decline of its total share and actually to generate increases in target segments of the market. Smaller media dollars thus concentrated on a clearly identified target outperformed the competition's bigger dollars.

Product Positioning

Another way to identify an opportunity is to build an entirely new product category. Take, for example, a new milk-additive drink, for which the initial entry was positioned as an all-purpose, all-occasion *drink*. The second major entry in the product category, however, was positioned by its sponsor as a "*food* for a specific meal occasion." The result: almost instantaneous success!

This new entry almost single-handedly created a new product category. The product was so successful that the marketing investment was returned in the first year that it was sold nationally. The successful company had identified a weakness in the competitor's product positioning and zeroed in on the most viable market segment.

Product Profile

An analysis of a product's profile may reveal an important weakness. This proved to be the case with the dominant brand in a beverage category, which held approximately a 45 percent share of the market. Historically, the brand had been a market innovator and, in effect, set the taste standard for the category.

A new entry was planned by a competitor whose strategy was to flank the leader with other product forms and with a different-tasting product. Extensive consumer taste testing was done to establish the leader's flavor profile. This enabled the newcomer to develop a product that had demonstrably superior consumer acceptance on the most important flavor characteristics. The new entry was positioned directly and successfully—against the leader's weaknesses.

A New Market Niche

Even in crowded market categories, an enterprising marketer may be able to find a new niche. A good example is the candy-bar market, which is highly fragmented. There are hundreds of different types sold through virtually every imaginable channel of distribution. And candy bars are consumed by all age groups in every demographic segment. Out of all of the different types, shapes and ingredients available to the candy buyer, it would seem virtually impossible to identify any consumer need not being filled.

But one company, after some intensive product development work met the challenge to identify a new niche for itself. Acting on this, the company sought, in effect, to expand the flavor spectrum previously occupied by three leading bars. By modifying the basic profile of these items, the company found it possible to formulate three new offerings.

Product Differences

One of the real challenges is making sure product differences are meaningful. It is possible to develop technology or manufacturing processes to incorporate something different into one's product. But the question is whether, in fact, that difference means anything.

Consider first an example of such a difference that did not matter. It involved the application of some truly revolutionary manufacturing technology that had been developed for one product category, but which was also applicable to another. The resulting difference in the second product was easy to demonstrate to the consumer; and the marketer was able to show the difference as well as to talk about it.

The company moved ahead swiftly into a test market. Several months later, following some costly test-market experience, it became obvious that consumers did not consider this new product form to be meaningfully dif-

ferent from existing forms. It did look different; but the results were the same. So, the key question is: Is the perceived difference in your mind or in the consumer's? Does the consumer really care?

One of the most dramatic examples of a successful product difference was that of the first toothpaste to obtain American Dental Association endorsement. This product was, in fact, different from any other then offered in the marketplace. The manufacturer was astute enough to take a very straightforward "news announcement" kind of approach to this product difference. The company was able to appeal to the real concern that consumers have about tooth decay. The endorsement of a prestigious organization for this product difference, and a straightforward advertising campaign, resulted in a dramatically successful product introduction. And, in this case, there was no question but that the product difference was meaningful.

Weakness in Distribution

In examining how products in a category are traditionally distributed, you may find that you can do it better and that the investment is worth it. One company made such a discovery with a simple product—a vegetable. Because of its perishable nature, this vegetable could only be sold canned or in the fresh form at limited distances from the growing source. Reviewing the situation, the company's management decided that there might be a marketing opportunity for the product in fresh form in those geographic areas beyond the reach of the normal growing areas.

The question to be answered was whether or not there was sufficient consumer demand to support the expanded marketing area made possible by some production technology available to the company. The product produced through this new technology was superior in terms of size, uniformity and appearance. Because it was possible to locate production sources closer to the marketplace, a continual supply of the fresh product could be made available.

Undertaking a project of this magnitude required a substantial investment, which management decided to make. The objective was to solve the distribution limitation under which competitors were operating and the traditional limitation on finished product quality. In this particular instance, both objectives were met.

Line Extension Opportunities

One of the most obvious methods of strengthening an existing product entry and attacking the competition is to flank it by flavor extensions and/or additional forms. A classic example of the success of this strategy has to do with dietary supplements. When first introduced, this particular item was positioned to the consumer as a medical product. Its initial success attracted literally hundreds of competitors. But the most successful new competitor did two things: (1) it positioned its product virtually as a cosmetic; and (2) it offered a wide variety of flavors. The result was that, over a period of time, the company was able to outflank the competition and eventually make its brand the leading one in the product category.

A walk down a supermarket aisle will reveal numerous examples of the strategy of flavor line extensions—in cake mixes, salad dressing, pet foods, barbecue sauces, frosting mixes, and so on. Howard Johnson's may have been one of the first to recognize its power in this regard, and many astute marketers have since applied the technique successfully.

Packaging Opportunities

Different is not necessarily better—either in products or packaging. Consumers, for example, become accustomed to certain kinds of packaging. There are many examples of packaging changes that have failed simply because they were too different or did not provide many meaningful advantages to the customer.

By contrast, one of the most dramatically successful packaging forms has been pouch packs. Today, of course, they may be taken for granted. But when they were first introduced, they were revolutionary because they provided consumers with premeasured quantities of such products as sauces, gravies and instant potatoes.

Soft-drink marketers are another group with success in changing their packaging. And they have done it in ways that provide meaningful advantages to consumers. Thus, packaging has evolved from cans requiring can openers, to throwaway pull tops, and now to pull tops that maintain product integrity while remaining a part of the package.

Demographics

For the marketer, there is more to demographic information than meets the eye. Purely demographic information—such as family size, age, income, and education—is not enough to identify competitive opportunities in today's complex world.

The problem is to understand the meaning of changes in our society and in life-styles, and how they are reflected in demographics. For example, the tremendous increase in the number of working housewives obviously has a positive impact on the sale of frozen convenience products. However, at the same time there is almost a countertrend of people returning to the kitchen where they seek to realize the satisfaction of preparing meals. The opportunity for a manufacturer, therefore, may be for products that are convenient to use but require sufficient involvement so that the person preparing the meal can have the gratification of contributing something personal to it.

The explosive growth of fast-food chains is one reflection of changing life-styles. People are delaying marriage and delaying having children; families are smaller; incomes are higher; people are traveling more; and more people are returning to colleges to complete or extend their educations. All of this contributes to the growth of the away-from-home meal market and, conversely, has had a negative impact on the food sales of supermarkets.

For their part, supermarkets are counterattacking with an expansion of their capabilities in offering delicatessen take-out food. They are providing consumers with another way to have fast hot or cold meals virtually prepared for them, but which they can then consume at home.

As helpful as quantitative demographic information can be for guidance, there are other ways to define or gauge consumers and their behavior. One leading research organization attempts to define people's behavior in terms of values—such as people who are conformists; people who are aggressive in seeking new experiences; people who are hedonists; people who are middle-of-the-road in terms of values; people who are moralistic in their viewpoint of society; and so on. Each group presents different kinds of marketing challenges.

It is also necessary for marketers to understand people's concerns about crime, inflation, changing morality, energy, the environment, and about the stability of their government and economic system. Reading the numbers alone will not assure meaningful insights into human behavior or into competitive opportunities.

Timing Is the Key

I have cited various possibilities for exploring and capitalizing on competitive opportunities. There is one additional and critical dimension to all this: timing. With the advantage of 20-20 hindsight, it is easy to see when somebody else's timing is off. *The Wall Street Journal* once noted that many of Chrysler's problems traced back to timing. Chrysler had correctly assessed the potential for compact cars, but it did so back in the late 1940's and early 1950's. The idea was right, but the timing was wrong.

There are many examples of products that failed, not because they were fundamentally unsound, but because they were ahead of their time. Conversely, of course, it is also critical to recognize when a product has failed to keep up with the demands of the marketplace.

Be Realistic

I would caution you to be realistic, especially about product differences. Do they exist only in your mind? If they are not meaningful to the consumer, can they be made to be? Ask yourself also whether a proposed packaging change really provides more convenience or simply results in a package that is more costly and difficult to use.

As managers, we all get caught up in the day-to-day pressures and find ourselves subject to the demands of sales, profits and return on investment. Nevertheless, if we are conscientious in looking at the competition and trying to identify its weaknesses, we should not neglect a look at those of our own company.

Try turning the whole situation around. Be the devil's advocate. Try being your own competitor and analyzing your own media strategy, product positioning, product profile, packaging, distribution and market demographics—as seen through the eyes of your competition. This could be the best way of all to avoid potential problems and to identify areas to attack competition.

Believe in the Better Way

Though it may sound naive in an age of cynicism, it is probably smart to believe that—with respect to anything—there is a better way of doing it. The fact is that ambitious people are finding opportunities in the most unlikely places every day.

Consider these examples:

• How many thousands of novels do you suppose have been written about American history? And yet John Jakes found a way to retell things in a manner that has made his works among the most commercially successful of the past decade.

• What can you do that is different with something as mundane as a coffee pot? Well, one creative businessman found out what could be done and began to market the Mr. Coffee Machine. Mr. Coffee moved to the forefront of the appliance category, the rebirth of the coffee pot.

• People have been wearing shoes of one kind or another for thousands of years. Other than cosmetic design changes, what else could possibly be new in this category? Somebody found it: The Famolare shoe. Enough people believe that it is different and better than other shoes, thus enabling the producer to build a successful company in a highly competitive industry.

Finding competitive opportunities is not only possible, it is also one of the things that makes the whole business effort worthwhile.

The Line vs. The Brand

Thomas W. Peterson
Vice President—Marketing
Vick Europe/Africa Division
Richardson-Vicks Inc.

Product-line management in the consumer products company, an evolution of brand management, frequently encompasses the planning and execution of marketing strategy for a group of products that share a common brand name. Effective product-line management has become a key part of strategic planning for more and more companies. Future product-line decisions can either provide the leverage needed for marketing success, or they can seriously damage a company's brand name and profits.

In exploring product-line management issues, we can start with some relevant questions:

- Why has product-line management become more important?
- How are packaged goods marketers using product-line management to leverage their sales?
- What are appropriate steps to be taken in formulating an overall strategy for a product line?

A cross-section of network television commercials and magazine ads for consumer packaged goods in a recent season provides clues to current trends. Of 295 such ads, 169—or 57 percent—featured more than one product in a line, or were for products which themselves had been introduced as line extensions. This is a much higher percentage than would have been found five or ten years ago.

What accounts for this trend to line marketing? It starts with a greater number of advertised brands in each major packaged goods category, year after year. This, in turn, translates into a tremendous increase in sheer advertising weight—the average consumer now is said to be exposed to up to 500 messages a day. And the demand for a share of the consumer's attention has driven advertising costs far beyond the general rate of inflation.

So, pity the poor marketer who wants to build awareness and an image for a new brand name. The company must pay inflated rates for advertising that is less effective because of the overall noise level. It is no wonder that the marketer often turns to an already-established name, hoping it will create faster recognition and a positive image transfer.

Examples

Consider some of the strategic objectives that line extensions are being used to fulfill. (As examples, I will refer to recent magazine advertisements for the products in question.) One of the most basic objectives is to provide flavor and form variety. Kool-Aid advertising from General Foods has long been an example of this technique. It is most often applied in a category where product usage is regular and frequent. The line extensions enable consumers to obtain variety without actually switching brands. Even the family dog gets sick of the same old thing all the time, and that is reflected in the three flavors of Gaines Top Choice promoted in a recent ad.

Another way in which marketers use line extensions is to keep their brands competitive in more than one discrete market segment. Advertising to the cigarette market provides numerous examples of this technique. Almost every new cigarette is launched in both regular and menthol versions. And that is not done to offer variety, like the previous examples cited. Instead it is done in recognition of the fact that menthol smokers are menthol smokers, and they will not be interested in a new brand at all unless they are offered a version tailored for them.

Similarly, Mellow Roast coffee was launched in both ground and instant forms, in order to be equally competitive in two discrete segments of the coffee market.

Gatorade from Stokely-Van Camp was originally available only as a single-strength liquid. But the obvious popularity of the powder form led Stokeley to introduce Gatorade Powder.

A third objective, closely related to the examples cited so far, is to extend an established brand name into a newly emerging consumer demand segment. Kent III is an attempt to provide a Kent entry into a very active low-tar cigarette segment. McNeil Laboratories launched Extra Strength Tylenol in order to compete in the growing extra-strength segment, with its high concentration of heavy users. All the media support was put behind Extra Strength, while McNeil relies on physicians to continue to promote the safety-oriented positioning of the original Tylenol. Incidentally, the extra-strength product is offered in tablet, capsule and liquid forms. This was a pretty complex job of market segmentation, but success in this case was quite obvious—Tylenol is now the number one analgesic brand in America.

Line extensions can also be used to widen a target audience. Bayer's Children's Aspirin offers a children's product with the well-known Bayer trademark. At the other end of the spectrum is Clairol's Silk and Silver, a hair-coloring line extension that appeals to the older woman.

Further, line extensions can be effectively used to blunt competitive attacks. Toni launched Light Waves to counter the tremendous success of Rave Home Permanent from Chesebrough-Pond's. This is a technique often used by established brands when a new competitor threatens their product category. They are combining a comparable consumer benefit with the equity of an established brand name.

Lastly, marketers use line extensions to enter entirely new categories while trading on the general credibility and acceptance of the established name. This is probably the most risky use of line marketing, since it is likely to dilute the sharp image of the brand name itself.

One example is Pitney-Bowes, originally known for its mail-handling equipment, which has expanded broadly into office equipment—particularly into copiers. A more closely related line extension is typified by Rave Hairspray. This product from Chesebrough-Pond's is trading on the success of Rave Home Permanent. It is interesting to note that the products themselves do not relate in any special way, but both are positioned as new hair-care products designed to capitalize on the current trend toward soft curls.

Pitfalls

Having seen all these marketers line-extending themselves into fame and fortune may give the impression that there are no pitfalls in making such a move, but there certainly are. Mismanagement of line marketing can have disastrous effects on the profit and loss state-

ment for the entire line and all its products. So anyone involved in line marketing decisions should be alert to several possible traps.

The first trap: line extensions can diffuse the image of the brand name, making it meaningless in the long run. Unless the brand name stands for something—a specific consumer benefit that is inherent in all the products of the line—it can change from an asset into a liability.

Second, the brand name can be extended into categories where it conveys no meaningful benefit. If you liked Vicks VapoRub, then you'll love Vicks Mouthwash, right? Wrong. My company actually tried that in the 1930's, but only in retaliation because Listerine had introduced a chest rub for colds. The image transfer did not work in either case.

There are also two other product-related reasons why line extensions can be dangerous. One is that closely linked line extensions limit the ability to improve or reposition one of the products, if that same improvement can not be made in the others.

The second reason is more obvious. One lousy product in your line can ruin the credibility of all the others. Product quality deficiencies always produce severe problems, but when the product in question is linked to all the others in your company by a common brand name, the risk is magnified tremendously.

The Magic Formula

Having noted the proliferation of line management, its uses and abuses, let us examine the possibilities for the actual planning of strategy. Is there one overriding guideline, one magic formula that can help you be a better planner of product-line strategy? Surprisingly enough, I think there is.

At the heart of every successful product-line marketing strategy is the recognition that the brand name must connote some kind of specific consumer benefit, and that benefit must be the same across all products within the line. All marketing efforts for every product in the line must support the common meaning of the brand name, and all products in the line must deliver on that implied benefit equally well. Take a simple example: Ivory Soap and Ivory Liquid from Procter and Gamble. These products are pure and mild and will thus be gentle to your skin. That is the promise that the Ivory name makes. Any marketing efforts for either one or both brands that did not support that basic promise would start to erode the clarity and power of the Ivory name. Further, the products must deliver equally well on that same promise, or users may be "turned off" from the entire line.

Obviously, then, the first step in the marketing planning process is to understand what your line's brand name means to consumers, both in the abstract and in the context of existing individual products. Of course, research techniques are available for this. The main message is that you must not assume that you know the answers. You may think your brand name stands for quality, integrity and modest price—but your name may also carry a connotation of "old fashionedness." It may be inexorably linked to one particular product benefit or to a particular type of product—like Xerox is to copiers. For example, why did Duncan Hines pancakes fall flat? The company found that its marketing efforts had built up a specific image of moist dessert items—an image that just could not be transferred to pancakes.

If you have spread the use of your brand name too far over the years, it may be much more general—and much less useful—than you think it has been. There are numerous trademarks out there that simply mean "from a well-known company." That is better than nothing, but do not count on it to sell a lot of product when your competitor is claiming more tangible consumer benefits.

Step two in the marketing planning process is to decide what you want that brand name image to be in the future, as it relates to your long-term marketing objectives. Essentially, you are setting an overall communications objective for your franchise. As you develop marketing plans, whether they are for advertising strategy changes or for new products to add to the line, you need to assess how each of these will affect the overall imagery of the brand name. Here, again, there are research techniques available, but in this instance they are much less precise. The real impact on your image—be it good or bad—may be so subtle that it will only appear after three or four years of national marketing. So, in most cases, you are down to old-fashioned judgment.

It is important to note that imagery transfer can work two ways when you launch a new product. The line's brand name helps a new product if its established imagery supports the main selling idea of the line extension. Conversely, the line extension itself can be used deliberately to change the meaning of the brand name. An interesting case study is that of the Cadillac Seville. Cadillac has always had an image, to me at least, of a huge luxury car. Somewhere along the line General Motors decided that the "huge" part of that image was not essential, and that a noticeably smaller Cadillac could succeed in today's market, as long as it still stood for luxury. As it turned out, they were correct. Seville has been successful in appealing to luxury import drivers, but the quality and luxury imagery of the big Cadillacs has apparently been untarnished.

Once you have defined the nature of the consumer benefit implied by your brand name, and decided what you would like it to be, the most critical determinant of line strategy is the relative importance of this overall brand-name benefit versus the benefits promised by the individual products. This is the key to your advertising and packaging strategy, and some examples will suggest what is involved.

If the various products in the line are very similar to each other—if they are only minor flavor or form variations—they can usually be advertised as a line. The overall selling proposition dominates the individual differences, as in advertising for Canada Dry mixers.

Another option under this circumstance is simply to advertise the leading version, without even mentioning the existence of other forms. Take recent ads for Crest Toothpaste. The importance of the traditional Crest decay prevention claim is so dominant that it was considered best to leave out any mention of a second flavor. Consumers in a store would certainly find out that there is also a mint-flavored Crest.

The opposite case frequently occurs, however: that is when the line contains products with strong, different consumer appeals, each with adequate media budgets. In this case, the overall brand name should be subordinated and de-emphasized. If it is used at all, it should be used as a secondary or implied selling point. For example, the name "Gaines" in Gravy Train ads appears only in the tiny print on the package itself.

In a third kind of situation, you may have a widely diverse line, with products and functions that vary, but where the potential for each product is too small to warrant advertising on its own. Here you may choose to skip the individual benefits and concentrate on establishing and maintaining a positive image for the brand name. Of course, the liability of this approach is that generalized statements tend to be less effective than specific consumer benefits.

Examples of several different strategies are sometimes found within a single line. Some of our Vicks products have sales volumes too small to warrant separate advertising, so we emphasize the Vicks name and use similar graphics. We count on the Vicks imagery—reliable, quality cold-care products—to sell them. On the other hand, where we have introduced major products with strong individual appeals, we have de-emphasized the Vicks name, both in labeling and advertising.

The final case in advertising strategy is an obvious one. What do you do with an established brand or proposed new product that has a very strong consumer promise not directly supportive of the imagery of the line? The answer here, clearly, is to launch it on its own or to throw it out of the line if it is already on the market. Resist the temptation to stretch the line trademark just to provide a little marketing top spin for a product.

For example, take Golden Lights, a highly successful cigarette introduced by P. Lorillard. It was introduced as a Kent line extension, but when it became apparent that it could stand on its own, Lorillard removed the Kent trademark. This prevented the rich-flavor position of Golden Lights from interfering with the original Kent positioning, and it cleared the way for Kent to promote a separate line extension—Kent III—in the super low-tar segment.

At this point, having laid down some foolproof guidelines, I feel strongly obliged to assure you that, like all rules in marketing, these have been broken successfully. For example, if you were launching a moisturizing hand cream called "Intensive Care," would you stick it with the brand name that stands for greasy old petroleum jelly—Vaseline? Somebody forgot to tell Chesebrough-Pond's, and they will probably never listen to us now.

Promotions

I have dwelt mainly on advertising positioning because I feel it is the most important element in consumer product marketing. But we should not forget trade and consumer promotion, in which you have a great deal more flexibility to use the line's leverage. As many Procter and Gamble coupon inserts demonstrate, a group of relatively disparate products—which do not even share a brand name—can be promoted to the consumer as a line. Again, however, remember that if a common brand name is used, both the copy and the nature of the promotion must support the basic imagery of the line. That is why, at Vicks, we are careful to use promotions and premiums that are related to the health and general welfare of the family.

In the trade promotion area, there are many opportunities to use the line technique to leverage dealer support. We encourage this kind of retailer ad through the use of preprinted "slicks." It is an example of a line effort that has generally more impact on the consumer than individual brand price listings. Some multiproduct displays of Vicks have more impact than we could hope to generate from a single-product activity.

If you are involved with one or more products that share a common name, you are in line management, whether you like it or not. If you are making decisions through a brand management system, you must be sure that the brand managers are sophisticated enough to understand the trade-offs they may have to make for the sake of line strategy. And you have to make sure that there is a strong marketing manager over the entire line, one who is willing to make the tough judgments and to provide the specific strategic direction required.

Optimal Breadth and Depth of the Line

Albert G. Munkelt
Senior Vice President—Marketing Planning
Foods Division
The Coca-Cola Company

PRODUCT LINES come in all lengths. Some are very short with two or three sizes, styles or flavors—such as Hellmann's, Skippy or Chicken of the Sea. Some are quite long—like Birdseye, Campbell's or Diet Delight—and a few go as far as several hundred items, like the Gerber baby products.

What is the optimal length of a product line? Is it 2 or 20 or 200? For each of the brands just cited, the current number of products in the line may be optimal. Obviously, no single length is optimal for all brands or trademarks, or in all circumstances.

No Single Answer

There are several reasons why this is so. In the first place, a majority of trademarks in the packaged foods industry—to which I will confine my examples, since it is the area with which I am most familiar—are confined by manufacturers to a single product category. This is only natural, as brand owners at the outset utilize their primary expertise and work with the raw material, manufacturing and distribution resources at their command. For example, most Hunt products are tomato-based; most Del Monte items are processed fruits and vegetables; Campbell's are primarily soup; and my company's brand, Minute Maid, comprises only fruit-based juices and ades.

On the other hand, some brands have moved beyond their basic specialty areas into entirely new product categories. The Morton frozen line had its foundation in meat pies and frozen food entrees. However, a few years back its sponsors ventured into the baked goods category with the introduction of frozen doughnuts. They were successful, and now they have extended that line to include honey buns, corn muffins, as well as several new varieties of doughnuts.

Take the case of Green Giant: For many years it was a brand of canned peas and corn niblets. Then it was expanded with other canned vegetable items—asparagus, string beans, mushrooms, and so forth. A few years ago, Green Giant made its move into the frozen food cabinet. First came a line of specialty vegetable items—such as brocolli spears in butter sauce, green beans with onions, cauliflower in cheese sauce. Basically, this is a natural extension. Later, the company made a much more significant extension with a frozen entree line including such products as stuffed green peppers, spaghetti and meat sauce, salisbury steak, and so forth.

The best example, although possibly unique, of great depth or wide extension across category lines is Kraft. Dominant in the dairy section with all kinds of cheeses and bottled fruit juice, Kraft is also big in several different dry grocery categories—jams and jellies, packaged dinners, salad dressing and mayonnaise, to mention a few. Kraft's optimal number is obviously a lot higher than most. What is the optimal length or breadth of extension for Morton, Green Giant, or Kraft? Obviously, it is different for each of these companies.

Procter & Gamble, incidentally, takes the opposite approach. For the most part, each single product is a single brand—Pringles, Puritan and Jif. For this strategy, the single product becomes the optimal number.

Thus, for some brands the optimal number may be very small. For others, like Kraft or Gerber, it may be much larger. It depends on the limitations of the particular product category, the financial and technical resources of the manufacturer, the company's marketing skill or strategy, and the brand's consumer acceptance.

Rules of Thumb

There are several considerations that a company should observe in the extension of its product line. First, of course, is profit. Ordinarily, a line extension should add profit to the brand or product line. (There are exceptions, which I will mention later.) Return on investment is also involved in this consideration. A new product, and even some line extensions, are big money investments today. As the product line is expanded item after item, the return may become smaller and smaller for each added entry. This will have a restrictive effect on the optimal size of the line.

Further, the line extension should enhance—or at least not detract from—the quality image of the brand. Each addition to the line should add value to the trademark and to the aggregate strength of the overall brand presence. An obvious objective, therefore, is to improve consumer awareness by increasing brand displays at retail outlets.

Yet another important consideration is credibility. The consumer has to believe that the new product, especially if it is outside the trademark's familiar category, reflects the expertise of the company or the brand owner. Many brands have been pushed into new product categories only to fail because the value perception of the original category could not be transferred to the new.

The foundation of Minute Maid was frozen concentrated orange juice; this is the product that established the trademark value and fine quality image. When it was introduced some 30 years ago, it filled a consumer need for a convenient, fresh-tasting citrus juice product. Later, it was logical to extend the line into closely related companion products like grapefruit juice, tangerine juice and pineapple juice. It was another step forward when we ventured into frozen citrus ades, the refreshment area. The consumer went along with us—Minute Maid was still in citrus and still credible. In logical progression, we moved from complete dependence on the frozen form into chilled juice products sold in the dairy case.

Now, for the first time, Minute Maid is on the dry grocery shelf with lemonade crystals. But observe: All of these 19 frozen, chilled or shelf items have one common denominator, fruit-based beverages.

A few forays into other fields using the Minute Maid trademark were without success. Examples include push-up bars, beef steaks, fruits and vegetables. For one reason or other, they did not make it. Maybe the plan was wrong, or maybe we did not properly address the consumer need or the consumer credibility for these extensions. I am not saying that a brand cannot take the long leap and move into new and different categories. But the financial investment, along with the marketing and sales effort, must be a lot higher in order to convince the consumer that the same relative brand quality and expertise prevail.

The criteria cited are all basic. At the same time, there are other important considerations for adding to the product line. One is to increase operational or plant efficiency—to secure maximum utilization of available plant-line time. Another consideration is advertising; the more products in the line with the same trademark, the more synergism in the advertising effort, leading to better advertising cost efficiency as well as greater advertising effectiveness.

Companies have been known, too, to add products to a line where no extra profit was programmed or anticipated in the near term. A short-term purpose, for example, may be to attract stockholders or to preempt a competitor in the protection of its position in a particular category.

On the other side of the equation, there are several factors that tend to limit the product line or to reduce its "optimal" length. First, the cost of fielding a new product these days is extremely high. Such an investment must be carefully calculated and the return on investment determined. Second, each sales force has its limitations, and consideration must be given to its capability to service the added line extension adequately. Third, though a new line extension may add value to the trademark, and even add sales revenue, will it directly cannibalize the line's existing products? Will it reduce the value of the line already on the shelf? If, for example, there is a line of nine flavors and now a tenth is added, the volume of two of these nine established flavors may be sufficiently reduced to become candidates for deauthorization.

The Retailer's Role

Mention of deauthorization reminds us of the retailer, who is most important to the success of any consumer product. In developing the optimal size of the product line, for example, the retailer must be taken into consideration.

Increasingly, the retailer today is serving as a funnel, or perhaps "filter" is a better word. The retailer is constantly besieged with new product offerings. Each year, for example, every food manufacturer has new line extensions to offer. Meanwhile, the retailer's overall shelf space remains finite. The retailer resists taking on additional items because there are only so many that can be accommodated in the warehouse, in the computer, and on the shelf.

When the retailer does take on the additional items, they normally must fit into the same shelf space previously allocated to the category. If you have a line of seven flavors and you offer three new ones, the retailer may try to put all ten into the space that originally accommodated only the seven. This raises an interesting question. Will the volume of some of the established products be so reduced that they become marginal to the retailer? Will the reduced space of each individual item lead to out-of-stocks and deauthorization and hence loss in volume and profit?

In a different situation, suppose that you have a line of 14 product flavors. And suppose that while every retailer in town carries eight of the 14, each of them has a different assortment. Does this lead to making each individual flavor that much weaker in the market? And to making the product advertising less efficient?

Retailers, who are the filters, are going to be critical in evaluating new product offerings to determine whether they should get through to their shelves and thus incur their investment in space and merchandising support. Here is where your brand's value comes into play. The retailer will take you on if your track record has been good, if you have a history of supporting your products to the consumer and making them move off the shelf and out of the store. If retailers feel that they are going to have to do the investing to make the product move, your chances are slim. It is critical for the manufacturer to establish a track record of being right, to build confidence in the brand's performance with the retailer.

If you have built a high-value image into your product line, you will reap many benefits. The retailer will tend to authorize your line extensions and provide additional display space for your brand. The added brand visibility will increase consumer impulse purchasing. In effect, the retailer will help your optimal number to increase.

Stewardship of the Line

To summarize: In adding products to the line to reach that so-called optimal length, corporate management is faced with an ever-increasing cost of new product introductions. When we add the cost of technical development, consumer research, package design, consumer sampling, advertising investment and sales and management involvement, the total cost is staggering. (Inciden-

tally, sometimes too much management time can be diverted to too small an item, a cost issue that should not be overlooked.)

In the stewardship of the line, management must evaluate not only the cost and its financial resources, but the capability of its technical, manufacturing, and marketing operations. At the same time, management must evaluate the probable reception that new offerings will get with the retailer and what competitive reaction can be anticipated. All of this will help establish the parameters of the product line, the optimal length. It is an evaluation that must be made *individually* for each situation. Each company must develop specific, parochial criteria in determining the length and category limitations of its product line.

Can we overwork the use of an individual trademark? Should we put all our eggs into one basket? Or should a second brand name be developed? When adding new products to the line, should certain other products be eliminated at the same time?

Nobody actually speaks this way; nobody really says we should not add a product to the line because we will exceed our optimal number. In the real world, we keep searching for new additions to the line that will be good for our brand; and when we find one that fits all of our specific criteria, we realize that the so-called optimal number can be increased.

So what is the right breadth and depth of the product line? By allowing for the considerations discussed, and by establishing criteria in keeping with your corporate objectives and resources, it is possible to determine whether your brand's length is in the optimal range.

Market Positioning Considerations

Linden A. Davis, Jr.
Senior Vice President
    and Director of Research
McCaffrey and McCall, Inc.

POSITIONING is most broadly defined as "matching a set of product attributes or benefits to a segment of the category market." Positioning is conceived by marketers as a *place* in the market—a place where a brand can maintain an identity of its own and, therefore, develop a consumer franchise with little or no competition from other brands.

Marketers often use the notion of positioning in the active sense, as in: "to position a brand" in one way or another. This is presumably a strategic activity. It aims the brand at the place or the position in the market that has been selected as an opportunity; and it is more appropriately called "positioning strategy."

There is nothing wrong with this concept so long as it is understood that it stops somewhat short of explaining what positioning actually is. At the bottom line, positioning is really a state of mind, a perceptual set in the minds of consumers. A practical concept of positioning must take both this perception and the consumers into account.

Ideally, this "perceptual" positioning (over which a marketer has only limited control) is a direct result of actions in support of the positioning strategy (over which a marketer has complete control). But it is not necessarily so. This is because a strategy goes through many filters before it is perceived. These include the product, the package, the pricing structure, the promotion mix, and, importantly, the advertising. In effect, the consumer is like a sponge, soaking up information from all such communication sources and generating his or her own perceptions.

An Example

An example is the positioning of Irish Spring. At the time that Colgate was developing and launching Irish Spring, the popular manufacturer's conception of the bar soap market was that it consisted of a complexion bar segment and a deodorant bar segment. Colgate Palmolive had entries only in the complexion bar segment, and had been losing its share. The deodorant segment was dominated by Armour-Dial and Procter and Gamble. Men were considered the principal users of deodorant soaps, and women of complexion bars. The logical positioning, which aimed at providing Colgate with an entry in the deodorant segment, was a "manly deodorant soap." Tactical considerations involved a unique, green, striated product (which supported a "double-deodorant" story) and a high-impact perfume.

Irish Spring, supported by heavy promotional spending, became a big success. Research indicated, however, that it was something more than a male deodorant soap. For one thing, it was used quite extensively by women. For another, it was perceived quite strongly as a *refreshing* soap, a new attribute in the bar soap market. Almost certainly, this was a new segment in the market. As evidence of this, consider the later launching of Coast with a refreshment and invigoration theme and just a hint of deodorant reassurance.

With Irish Spring, Colgate got something it had not bargained for. Fortunately, it turned out happily. The point is that consumers "positioned" Irish Spring in a way, I am sure, that was much different from what was intended. Colgate's positioning strategy resulted in a different *perceptual positioning*. In this case and always: It is consumers who position. To lose sight of this consideration—even early on—is a big mistake. The key question is: How will this product be perceived?

Research and Analysis

Numerous methodologies are used in the search for viable positioning strategies. They range from the qualitative (focused groups and the like) to such exotic forms of analysis as cluster analysis, multidimensional scaling, and other multivariate approaches. Each has its adherents who will give you a host of reasons why it is best. My own preference leans to the tried-and-true cross-tabular analyses. My experience has been that these straightforward approaches, such as in problem detection, have more new-product successes to their credit than any of the supersophisticated ones. This is only an opinion and I have no statistics to back up that statement. However, I believe that the most useful positioning information can be obtained by going back to very basic research.

In the quest for a positioning strategy a logical question is: What should be covered in a market study to increase the odds of new-product success? A valuable approach, which takes an extraordinary amount of discipline, is to toss out the window all previous assumptions about a product category. I would urge you to do this even if you have been marketing in the product category for 50 years. Let's face it: Many product categories, and many so-called segments, are based on definitions fashioned by manufacturers, not consumers. I suggest that we not constrain ourselves to these a priori assumptions, but rather turn our attention directly to actual consumer behavior.

Thus, an extremely valuable first step in the search for positioning opportunities is to consider the market from the point of view of consumer behavior. This approach not only frees us from self-imposed category and segment definitions, but also captures the consumer perceptions that are critical to the understanding of positioning. What consumers actually do reflects their perceptions and understandings of the various categories and brands. In short, consumer behavior determines existing positionings.

An example is the packaged rice category. From the manufacturer's perspective, this category is probably divided into at least three market segments: instant rice, raw rice, and flavored rices. I submit that the consumer rarely considers rice as a category, except possibly for buying it. In using rice, the consumer probably tends to consider rice as one alternative in what might be called the "nonvegetable, meat supplement" market. This considerably broader behavioral market includes potatoes, pasta and macaroni, and—in recent years—the stuffing mixes. All of these categories, and the various brands within them, compete for use in this area; and the consumer *perceives* them as interchangeable. Only rarely would a housewife serve several of them at the same meal.

Investigation of the behavioral market is not difficult. It requires finding the answers to such "what" questions as:

(1) *What* is the general behavioral area?
(2) *What* do consumers use in this general behavioral area?

For example, if we wanted to develop a positioning for a new shampoo, I would not recommend doing a "shampoo study." Instead, I would begin by finding out "what people put on their heads."

The next consideration—after identifying the general behavioral area, and the relevant competing brands (and categories)—is to find answers to such questions as:

(1) *How* are the brands used?
(2) *When* are the brands used?
(3) *Where* are the brands used?

These questions refer to the purposes that the consumer is attempting to satisfy by the use of the brands and/or categories chosen. This area of market research, though largely uninvestigated, can be extremely valuable. To illustrate: For years the market for analgesic products had been perceived by manufacturers as for muscle aches. However, a diary study of external analgesics uncovered that about one-third of Ben-Gay's usage, and over 50% of its volume, went for arthritis relief. This was a hitherto unknown purpose for which Ben-Gay was being used. McCaffrey and McCall developed a separate market strategy for each of the two ailments—muscle aches and arthritis. As a result, a stagnant brand leapt forward with renewed vitality.

To restate this point: *A segment of consumers positioned Ben-Gay as an arthritis treatment.* Thus, consumers position brands according to their needs. Their behavior reflects this positioning. Asking the questions how, when and where can identify the purposes for which they use each brand.

The "Why" Questions

Extending this concept just one step further, the next consideration is to get at the whys and wherefores of the brand applications to the uncovered purposes. In my opinion, however, most attitudinal work today does not go deep enough and is often downright misleading. Consumers express their brand attitudes or perceptions according to the use context with which they have experience. Without first identifying the segmentation of brands and purposes, direct attitudinal comparisons may well be inappropriate.

For instance, is it appropriate to compare the attitude profiles of Chivas Regal Scotch users to those of Canadian Club? Maybe yes and maybe no. What first has to be determined is whether both brands are used for identical purposes. If Chivas Regal is sipped on the rocks for *relaxation* and Canadian Club is drunk with water for *refreshment,* it is clearly inappropriate to draw comparisons. But if both brands share the purpose of relaxation, then comparisons may be meaningful.

Therefore, wherever possible, attitudinal information

should be developed according to the purposes of use. By this I do not mean simply cross-tabulating a set of attitudinal data by purpose of use, but rather obtaining attitudinal measurements according to each purpose. In all this, information on consumer satisfaction is vital for uncovering holes or opportunities in the market.

Another consideration is why consumers are not using a particular brand or product category. Perhaps large segments of the population are currently using another category to satisfy certain purposes that your category of interest is capable of satisfying. It is possible that they do not use your category because of attitudes or perceptions that could be changed. Once all of these areas have been investigated, it is a simple analytical task to find out who—by customer class—is using the different categories and brands in the various ways examined.

Targeting: The Final Step

Identifying the target audience should follow the behavioral investigation, rather than precede it. In my opinion, selecting a target segment in advance is one of the most common mistakes in new-product development. Without first obtaining a thorough understanding of the structure of the behavioral market—including the needs and purposes that consumers are attempting to satisfy and their beliefs about current products in satisfying these needs—the process of market segmentation is merely shooting in the dark. Since positioning demands that one take the consumer (or market target or segment) into account, a shaky segmentation yields poor positioning strategies. As I have tried to demonstrate, starting with an understanding of consumers' behavior minimizes the chances of mistakes.

Successful Market Positioning—One Company Example

Samuel R. Gardner
Vice President—Marketing
Retail Food Group
Kraft Inc.

LIKE MANY OTHERS, the dairy business represents a far different marketing climate than it did only some ten to twenty years ago. In those earlier days, success was pretty much based on the ability of the many local processors to establish strong distribution franchises in their own trading areas. Consumer demand was traditionally quite strong and stable, and federal and local regulations were basically protectionist. Food retailers, for the most part, had not yet decided to invest heavily in processing their own milk and related by-products.

By the 1960's, a lot of this had changed. Major food retailers, capitalizing on the mass demand and high turn-over of these products, had started moving into the dairy business. And through networks of centralized, controlled distribution, they were able to market their own labels more efficiently than could those of many of the local or regional suppliers.

The consumer climate was changing, too. Dietary concern, new lifestyles, and the explosion of new products—along with the rising consumer demand for other beverages and snacks—all tended to have a depressing effect on per capita consumption of milk and ice cream.

Ironically, the very regulatory climate that earlier had helped to maintain the franchise of the independent brand producers now acted as a deterrent to the kind of marketing innovation that was called for to combat the new competitive situation. Ice cream is a typical example, since it is a product category where most of the ingredients and methods of processing have been standardized by the Food and Drug Administration for many years. Until the 1960's, the marketing strategies and product positionings of most ice cream marketers had developed along the lines of either a pricing incentive of one form or another, or some kind of inflated claim of superior quality.

By the late 1960's, Kraft realized that the alternative of competing primarily on a price appeal was not an acceptable strategy for long-term growth and profitability in this business. The company also realized that something more was needed than simply an overall quality umbrella based on the traditional reputation of a product's brand name and on its distribution network. To be successful, Kraft knew that somehow it would have to convince the retail trade that its profitability in ice cream would be maximized by offering the consumer a *mix* of premium priced brands along with their own lower priced private labels. Of course, this whole mix argument rested upon one critical assumption: That we could, in fact, develop and successfully market the kind of products that would generate consumer demand for reasons not related primarily to a low price.

Someone familiar with successful packaged-goods marketing techniques may find nothing especially startling in this approach. But ten years ago, and even today to a large degree, this approach has been a revolutionary departure from the marketing philosophy that existed for a long time in the dairy industry.

The Breyers Story

In the late 1960's, Kraft was marketing an ice cream called Breyers in the New York, Philadelphia, and Baltimore-Washington areas. It has always been a fine product, made virtually in the same way for more than a 100 years. Like most other well-known local brands, Breyers ice cream had always been positioned very generally as a premium quality product, with the reputation of its brand name offering the primary difference from other brands. But in the 1960's, a significant difference in the way Breyers ice cream was formulated became the focus for a new positioning strategy.

As spelled out in a pledge of purity that appears on every carton, Breyers ice cream does not contain *any* kind of artificial flavoring, nor does it contain any added coloring. And, more significantly, it does not contain any stabilizers or emulsifiers which tend to provide a degree of creaminess that is just not possible without their aid.

The nonstabilized formulation of Breyers provides what we in the business call a better "flavor release" and distinctive "mouth-feel." This basic product difference triggered a whole new approach to promoting ice cream. For instance, in Breyers peach ice cream, only four simple ingredients are used: milk, cream, sugar and peaches. Nothing else is added—a product attribute that did not have much meaning or exposure only a decade or so ago.

In those days, the consumers' interest in natural foods was just beginning to emerge as a positioning consideration; and very few, if any, marketers were making much noise about it. An advertising campaign was developed that targeted the Breyers product as "*The* All-Natural Ice Cream." This positioning was deliberately designed to be more of an ingredient story than to have a health or ecological appeal. Copy reported on the quantity as well as the quality of the ingredients (e.g., Breyers takes more than a pound of peaches to make a half-gallon of peach ice cream).

This new Breyers positioning caught on quickly, and in three years sales in its traditional marketing areas had doubled. It was then realized that this strategy could be an effective means of introducing the brand into new markets where the all-natural positioning had not yet been used to its fullest. This was a great idea, but how could we face up to the challenge of attempting to justify the introduction of a new premium ice cream, Breyers, when we were already well-represented in these markets by Sealtest, another premium quality brand? Why would the trade want to make room for both of our premium ice creams, especially when they were already having trouble accepting the rationale for allowing even one of them to compete with their own label?

And what about the consumer? If we sell the consumer on the merits of Breyers as being the best quality product, what do we say about Sealtest? That it is almost as good? Might we really be only competing with ourselves for the same customer? And possibly even confusing the consumer about which one is really the better?

In coming to grips with these and other somewhat difficult strategic questions, a solution evolved that led to the creation of what was called "The Premium Ice Cream Program." Basically, this is a three-brand marketing strategy that recognizes several key consumer purchase and demand considerations that are important to the ice cream business.

First of all, we knew that the success of the Breyers "all-natural" appeal was not just limited to consumers with higher incomes, who could afford to pay a premium price. Our experience in New York and Philadelphia in-dicated that this particular all-natural product positioning was effective among all demographic groups. But what about the considerable number of ice cream consumers who could care less about the appeal of naturalness, but who want something they feel is special in an ice cream?

The Sealtest Story

To appreciate the development of Kraft's Sealtest positioning, it is important to know that many Americans have come to believe that ice cream from an ice cream parlor is somehow superior in quality to products distributed in supermarkets. Right or wrong, this perception persists for many; and, in fact, has been flourishing lately with the increasing number of retail ice-cream-parlor establishments opened during the past years. It was also interesting to us that, during this period, total sales of ice cream sold through supermarkets had been declining, while that sold through ice cream parlors was increasing. It was not all in the form of cones either.

The well-entrenched, top-quality image of the ice cream parlors' ice cream has been responsible, no doubt, for the fact that a surprisingly high tonnage of it has been sold to consumers in the form of packaged half gallons, usually at a price of up to two, and sometimes three, times higher than supermarket distributed half gallons, including Sealtest ice cream. Since blind product testing confirmed that Sealtest compared favorably on taste with "ice-cream-parlor" ice creams, and since this meant that we could then have a potentially meaningful price-value advantage over these products (which were competing directly against our customers, the supermarkets), an exciting positioning strategy presented itself for the Sealtest brand.

So Sealtest became "The Supermarket Ice Cream With That Ice Cream Parlor Taste." This positioning now gave us a strong sales argument for the trade, as well as a powerful consumer appeal that, we hoped, would be compelling for its own merits, yet would not necessarily conflict with the natural-ingredient appeal developed for Breyers.

To execute the Sealtest taste strategy, we created dramatic TV advertising featuring hidden-camera interviews with real people who, after testing both products, could not tell the difference. This advertising, as well as quality packaging, helped to build the believability of this positioning. It had really worked, thanks mainly in the final analysis, to the performance of the product.

An Ice Milk Brand

Finally, our Premium Ice Cream Program recognizes the relatively small, but still very meaningful opportunity to attract consumers of ice milk, who buy this product either because they cannot or do not want to pay the price for fine ice cream. The problem is that, as a category, ice milk traditionally has not been formulated to measure up to ice cream. The ice milks are cold and sweet; and they are a lot less expensive than ice cream. But, by and large, that's it! So-so flavor and so-so texture. A very unexciting product category from a marketing development standpoint.

We saw an opportunity to capitalize on this situation by developing a premium ice milk brand with a lot of the texture and taste qualities typical of ice cream. Such a product would be targeted directly at the existing ice milk user but, strategically, would also become a viable alternative for consumers of lower priced, lower quality ice creams. Since this positioning called for a superior tasting ice milk, premium pricing was required, even though it would still be established below the pricing of both Breyers and Sealtest ice creams.

Such a product was developed and marketed under the Light n' Lively name, which was nicely suited for this brand since all ice milk, by law, is required to have less butterfat than ice cream. The minimum for ice cream is 10 percent; for ice milk, it is between 2 and 7 percent. Light n' Lively has been formulated to support a claim of "Less than Half the Fat of Ice Cream."

Also, with the Light n' Lively name came the added advantage of being able to benefit from any synergistic effect of the promotion and awareness of what is happening with all of the other low-fat products bearing the Light n' Lively name—such as fluid milk, process cheese, low-fat yogurt, and cottage cheese. Advertising stressed an "ice creamy ice milk" texture claim, since research had told us that, after price, this is the single best motivating claim area for ice milk users. It also happens to be the positioning that is most likely to be able to justify a premium price.

Now, A Complete Line

With the addition of the two ice cream products, Kraft would have a line of packaged frozen dessert brands that could maximize profitable sales both to the consumer and to the trade. Each would have its own distinctive niche in the marketplace; and, in total, could now provide a more complete marketing program, since the three brands would be not so much *competitive* as *compatible* with each other. For us, this has been the magic of this three-brand positioning strategy.

Since the early 1970's, ice cream consumption in the United States has been relatively flat. In the five years following the inception of the program, total sales of packaged ice cream increased about 5 percent. During this same period, Breyers sales increased over 50 percent overall, with a 17 percent increase in the markets where Breyers ice cream had been a well-established brand for many, many years. And on top of this, Sealtest sales jumped another 23 percent. As for the ice milk situation, this business had also remained relatively flat. However,

Light n' Lively, as an integral part of the Premium Ice Cream Program, jumped 45 percent during the same five years.

The program worked in an extremely difficult marketing climate, but the positioning for these three brands was right. I am happy to add that, while some of our competitors have attempted to emulate our positioning to one degree or another, the total impact of the Kraft program is still relatively unusual and highly successful in this business.

A Carryover to Cottage Cheese

We are now in the process of using the same basic positioning concepts that have worked so well on frozen desserts to other selected dairy product categories with which Kraft is involved. For instance, in cottage cheese, another large tonnage market like ice cream with sales around $1 billion a year, Kraft has developed what we call "The Premium Cottage Cheese Program."

The primary consumer appeal in this food category has always been diet—the desire for lower calorie food alternatives at mealtime. It is a fact that all cottage cheese can satisfy this desire to one degree or another, but the Light n' Lively brand has been deliberately targeted right at this important hard-core diet appeal, since it is specially formulated as a 1 percent low-fat product. The so-called "regular" cottage cheeses are standardized by law to contain a minimum of 4 percent fat—four times greater than Light n' Lively cottage cheese.

Today, Light n' Lively is the leading brand among low-fat cottage cheeses. So our "Premium Cottage Cheese Program" is well represented as far as a specific diet positioning is concerned. But while this diet appeal may be the prime purchase motivation for most users, the market for the so-called low-fat cottage cheeses still amounts to only about 15 percent of total category sales, even though it is growing faster than the regular type.

As with many food products, there tends to be a range of taste or flavor appeals beyond price that offer possibilities to segment consumer demand. In the case of cottage cheese, product characteristics such as creaminess, freshness, texture and curd size can all be important purchase considerations. So in addition to the Light n' Lively diet-oriented product offering, this program features two other brands which are positioned to satisfy a particular taste appeal that is meaningful for this category. Our Sealtest Brand is a "regular" (or 4 percent butterfat) type of cottage cheese that is specially formulated with a sweet-cream dressing in both small and large curd varieties, as well as some flavors (which tend to be a minor factor in total demand).

In all of these forms, the brand is deliberately positioned to appeal to the widest segment of potential buyers since it is a relatively fresh and sweet-tasting product whose flavor is, we feel, so pronounced that it is able to stand out from all the other foods that research tells us are usually eaten along with cottage cheese. This is a product appeal that certainly should be meaningful to most category users, particularly those who are not really crazy about cottage cheese and tend to be using it only for diet-related reasons.

A third product in our program is Breakstone's cottage cheese, which is deliberately formulated to be somewhat drier and more tangy flavored than the Sealtest brand. It is also a 4 percent fat type of cottage cheese which is marketed in both small and large-curd styles. Breakstone's brand is also positioned as a premium priced brand, and is especially popular in the East where a number of Breakstone's products have had a large following going back, like Breyers ice cream, for more than a 100 years. It tends to appeal more to the people who want a very distinctive product—what we refer to as a "traditional" type of cottage cheese. And unlike our other two brands, Breakstone's is formulated to be completely natural.

Thus, here again, a multibranded, segmented positioning approach has been able to maximize Kraft's opportunity within the total category—in this case, cottage cheese. In all of this positioning, the key has been to identify or, sometimes, to create meaningful and distinctive consumer appeals that can be well satisfied by products that can deliver value regardless of the required pricing.

Critical Trade-Offs

William T. Moran
President
Moran, Inc.

THE NECESSITY FOR TRADE-OFFS is one of the unpleasant facts of life. The notion that we usually have to give up one thing to get another certainly is true in the management of consumer product lines—whether guiding an existing line; making additions to a line; dropping items from a line; introducing completely new products; or creating entirely new lines.

Major trade-off choices often relate to financial efficiency, management efficiency, marketing experience and know-how, or consumer appeal. Trade-offs in financial efficiency, for example, hinge on such questions as whether to utilize present productive capacity or to invest in new capital equipment. There are related trade-off decisions affecting both the financial and production areas, such as between two products with respect to resulting economies of scale when available resources force a choice. Still other trade-off decisions concern energy efficiency, employee relations, or, inceasingly, alternatives in the physical distribution of marketed goods.

In the Western world, it was long assumed that if consumption were stimulated, production would follow and everyone would get richer. We are backing away from this idea these days, and our primary concern is increasingly with production. One consequence is that product-line management in the future will have to seek bigger markets and to make decisions among groups of products rather than one at a time. There will still be market segmentation, of course, but there surely will be less of it. And the segments will usually be of more fundamental types than before.

Also, there will be fewer complicated attempts, I believe, to see if one can discover a promising psychological segment out there in the market. Instead, marketers will be dealing with more basic notions in the marketplace. In particular, they are going to be looking for economies of scale in their operations and for ways to be more cost-competitive.

Not only will it be important to be able to compete on the basis of cost relative to your direct competitors, but—something so often neglected—it will possibly be even more important to be cost-competitive relative to your *indirect* competitors. In recessionary times of the 1970's, there was a great deal of shifting of consumer dollars across product categories. Indeed, diverse products whose sponsors had not recognized that their offerings were competing against each other at all, were in fact doing so.

Evaluating Prospective Market Opportunities

That cross-elasticities exist between what appear to be different product categories is poorly understood, although it can be highly relevant in examining prospective markets for entry, or products that a manufacturer is thinking of adding to or dropping from a current line. Most managements know very little about such matters as what their indirect competition is and how this should influence decisions regarding product-line proliferation.

A focus on categories of product *usage,* for example, can offer a different way of thinking about markets from usual industry classifications. The A.C. Nielsen classifications of product categories—familiar to consumer goods marketers—really are industry classifications based upon common production processes or raw materials rather than consumer classifications. Often, things that seem "alike" because they are in the same product category, really are not; and—more important—some things that lie outside of a product category may seem unalike, although in a consumer competitive sense they really are to some extent alike in that they exhibit a substantial degree of cross-elasticity.

There are fascinating examples of this phenomenon. Take the toilet soap market, which really is not a single, homogeneous market. Lux and Lifebuoy, for example, do not compete very directly in the same market, although each is given a share of the "toilet soap" market in Nielsen reports. Actually, one of them enjoys a big share of the shower-soap market and a negligible share of the face-soap market, while the situation for the other brand is the reverse. Thus, they are used in different situations and for different purposes.

By contrast, consider the soup business—canned soup, in particular—where the alternative product choices for consumers are not necessarily other soups. Often, the most important competition for canned soup may be some other food, such as a peanut-butter sandwich or, on a cold day, a cup of hot chocolate.

It is not always apparent or self-evident what the "market" for a product or individual brand really is. In thinking about product-line proliferation, therefore, it is a good idea to view the matter in terms of usage situations and to develop mixed strategies for the entire line. This will enable you to hedge your bets. Increasingly, companies hereafter will be employing mixed strategies to minimize the risks that everything will go wrong at the same time. With an uncertain future, that has to be a major consideration.

There are other strategic classifications which are profitable ways to define markets. I call them "consumption markets." Profit leverage can be obtained by directing corporate strategy at consumption markets defined in terms of: distribution systems; end uses; situations and occasions; objective product attributes; functional product attributes; and characterizational attribute association.

Multiproduct Strategy Issues

Matchups of various factors I have mentioned—marketing know-how, product usage situations, and cross-elasticities between products—bear on management's strategy decisions. Take the situation at General Motors, for example, where the marketing of three different products—Chevrolet, Buick and Oldsmobile—calls for the same general marketing know-how and does not strain management by forcing its marketers into areas with which they are unfamiliar. Similarly, the usage situation is the same when someone is driving one of these products and not the others. And, of course, the cross-elasticity between the three is high as a result. That is, if GM sells a Chevrolet, it is less likely to sell that customer a Buick, and vice versa.

Another type of situation is that exemplified by General Mills in its efforts to sell Hamburger Helper and to run the Red Lobster Inn chain. These two activities call for different kinds of marketing know-how; and, of course, the distribution systems are entirely different. Still, the usage situation is the same: It is mealtime. As a result, there is medium cross-elasticity between them.

RCA has a somewhat similar situation with its NBC television network and videodisc business. There exists some cross-elasticity between the two, and they call for different kinds of marketing know-how. But the consumer usage situation remains pretty much the same.

Yet another company, The Stanley Works, faces a quite different situation in that it sells hammers, screwdrivers, and saws. Like those in the Chevrolet, Buick and Oldsmobile mix, these items call for similar marketing know-how and a similar usage situation. But when you sell somebody a hammer, you are more likely—rather than less likely—to also sell that same individual a screwdriver. So, here is a product line with medium cross-elasticity between offerings; but in this case it is a *plus* relationship, since the sale of one actually increases rather than reduces the probability of making a sale of the other two.

There are cases where different markets for products of a company require different kinds of marketing know-how, where the products are employed in different usage situations, and where the cross-elasticity is very low—such as the market dynamics Chesebrough-Pond's faces in selling its Ragu tomato sauce and its Erno Laslo skin-treatment products. (Examples cited here are simply for illustrative purposes; and, obviously, the items mentioned are not always treated by the seller as part of the same product line.) The sale of one company item in such instances does not materially affect the probability of the sale of the other company offering to the same customer.

Optimal marketing strategy under such varying conditions will differ from company to company, and it will depend on such things as the degree of risk taking associated with its style of management; how much confidence management has in the forecast of future happenings in the market; and the kinds of marketing talent and financial resources available to support the marketing effort.

Repeat Purchase Rate

In building new-product strategy in the consumer market area, the repeat purchase rate is one of the first things to examine when screening product categories as possible contenders for new entries by the company. Admittedly, the repeat purchase rate does not apply meaningfully to some consumer product categories, like refrigerators. Where the purchase cycle is exceptionally long, the repeat purchase rate is not a relevant statistic. For these we employ another analogous statistic.

But in many product markets, measures of repeat purchases can be very instructive. For one thing, they reflect a direct analogue of market concentration. Take, for example, the two hypothetical brands referred to in Exhibit 1. They both are in the same product category, which has an average of ten purchase cycles—that is, ten unit purchases per category customer—a year. (For the category, annual sales units per 100 customers is 1,000.)

Exhibit 1: Repeat Purchase Rate for Typical Brands

Measure	Brand A	Brand B
Average purchase cycle for category	10 units per year	10 units per year
Annual category unit sales per 100 customers	1,000	1,000
Brand share of market	10%	10%
Brand sales per 100 category customers	100	100
Brand purchasers per 100 category customers	25	100
Brand unit sales per 100 brand customers	400	100
Brand share of market among brand customers	40%	10%

Exhibit 2: Payout Periods for a Typical Brand

Measure	Value for Brand C
Average purchases for category per year (no.)	10
Brand C share of market (%)	10
Unit gross margin ($)	0.10
Marketing expense, present customer ($)	0.30
Marketing expense, new customer ($)	0.70
Purchases of Brand C per year, present customer (no.)	4
Payout period, present customer (no. months)	9
Payout period, new customer (no. months)	21[a]

[a] If the new customer exhibits the same repeat purchase rate as the present customer.

Further, since the market share of each of the two charted brands is 10 percent, each obviously is selling 100 units a year per 100 *category* customers. But they accomplish this in very different ways. The marketer of one brand achieves its total by selling its 100 units to 25 people over the course of a year. The other one accomplishes the same thing by selling 100 units to 100 people over the course of a year. Thus, the unit sales per 100 *brand* customers in the case of Brand A is 400 per year; and in the case of Brand B, it is 100 per year. Both brands have a 10 percent share of market defined as a single category; and yet they are also very different: Brand A has a 40 percent share of category usage among those people who buy that brand at all, whereas Brand B only has a 10 percent share among those who do so.

Brand A has an obviously higher repeat purchase rate, with its business more concentrated among fewer people. This relationship is important because of the way in which the economics of the repeat purchase rate—or market concentration—works. Assume that the marketer of a hypothetical brand purchased on average ten times a year has a market share, again, of 10 percent, and a unit gross margin of 10 cents. Such a company will spend about 30 cents per customer to hold the present collection of consumers buying its brands (see Exhibit 2). That is the cost of its total marketing program over the course of a year divided by its present customer base. (The company will necessarily spend a great deal more than this, relatively, in switching others into the franchise who have not previously been purchasers of the brand.)

Suppose that the company on average sells four units of its brand each year to a present customer, and the associated payout takes nine months. (This is not atypical, since sellers often spend the first nine months or so just trying to get up to break-even, and they have only the two or three months at the end of the year in which to make their entire profit.) But the payout period for *new* customers is rarely as short as this. With them, payout takes many times longer because more money has been spent to capture them. It could take even longer than the 21 months indicated in Exhibit 2, because the premise of the arithmetic here is that the repeat purchase rate will be the same among newly acquired customers as it is among customers in the present customer franchise base. If that is not actually so, then it will take longer still to gain payback from the purchases made by the new customer. In short, then, we see that a present customer is much more valuable in the near term than a new customer.

It follows that, given two brands with the same share of market, the one having the higher repeat purchase rate, or the higher concentration of its customers, will be the more profitable. Its sponsor will need to spend less money in maintaining its customer franchise. The other competing brand will have to spend constantly to maintain a flow of new triers, as people go in and out of its franchise. (Thanks to the economic logic of gross margins, it is a rare company that can afford to maintain market share for a brand by expending significantly higher support funds for any protracted period than do its competitors.)

As it turns out, the repeat purchase rate within any product category displays a very systematic relationship to brand-share purchases. Exhibits 3, 4, 5, 6 and 7 show plottings of real data for some five product categories in a period of the 1970's. The last-time-purchased (LTP) scale on the left refers to the percentage of category buyers who bought the indicated brand on the last occasion when they made a purchase in this category. Each of the dots represents a different brand in the category. You will see, for example, that one brand accounted for 25 percent of the Category A purchases that had been bought "last time" (the last purchase made in the category by each category purchaser). That is the next to the biggest share. A second brand garnered an even larger share—37 percent—of last-time purchases in Category A. Last-time share of purchasers is closely equivalent to share of unit sales volume for the category.

Exhibit 3: Percentages of Buyers' Last-Time Purchases and Repeat Purchases of Selected Brands, Product Category A

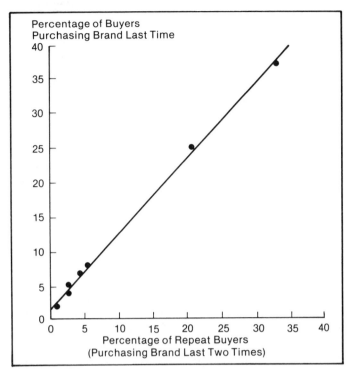

Exhibit 4: Percentages of Buyers' Last-Time Purchases and Repeat Purchases of Selected Brands, Product Category B

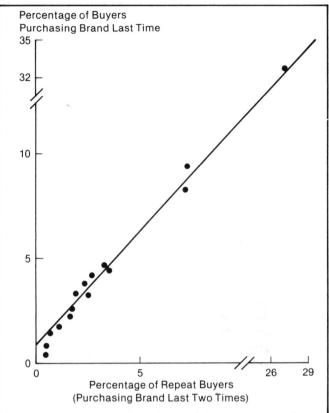

Exhibit 5: Percentages of Buyers' Last-Time Purchases and Repeat Purchases of Selected Brands, Product Category C

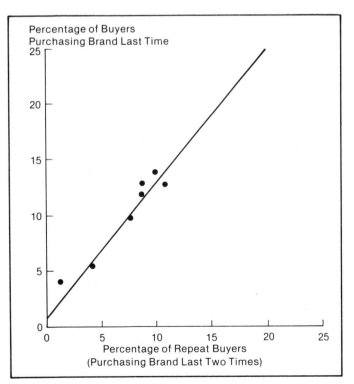

Exhibit 6: Percentages of Buyers' Last-Time Purchases and Repeat Purchases of Selected Brands, Product Category D

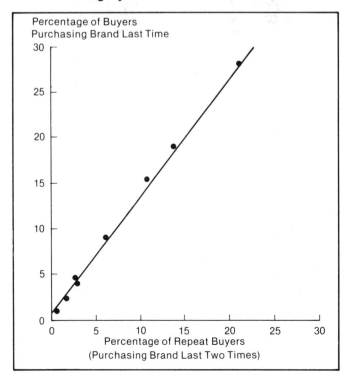

Exhibit 7: Percentages of Buyers' Last-Time Purchases and Repeat Purchases of Selected Brands, Product Category E

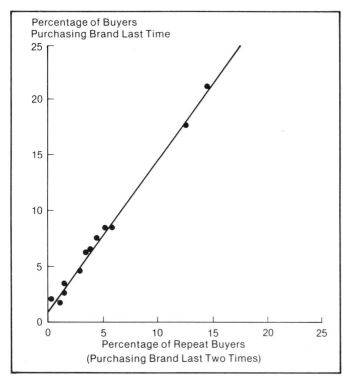

The bottom scale in Exhibits 3 through 7 refers to the percentage of persons who bought the indicated brand on both of the last *two* occasions when making purchases in that category. So, in the case of the brand bought last time by 25 percent of the Category A buyers, about 21 percent of Category A buyers bought it both on that occasion and on the time before last. What is important to note is the remarkably systematic relationship obtaining, with every one of those dots—separate brands—falling almost exactly on a straight line for the category. In fact, the presence of this kind of pattern is one of the operational definitions of whether or not you have isolated a real product category—i.e., one where the brands are in direct competition. And in all five of the categories illustrated in Exhibits 3 through 7 the plotted dots do fall virtually on a straight line.

Among other things, this tells us that the marketing costs on a brand have to be competitive. That is, you cannot afford to maintain your share of market with a higher proportional level of occasional switchers than is true for the sellers of other brands of comparable size in the category. Because switches cost more and reward less, no competitor can long maintain such a situation, and each will tend to drop back to the relationship characteristic of all the other brands in the market—with respect to the share of purchases and the rate of repeat purchases.

Exhibit 8, which summarizes the situation for all five brands, reveals that those five diagonal lines on earlier charts all differed in their slopes. As can be seen, in order

to maintain a 20 percent share of last-time purchases within Category E, you will have to have about 13 percent of the consumers buying your brand both last time and the time before last. This translates (13 divided by 20) into a 65 percent repeat purchase rate, which is typical for a 20 percent share brand in that product category. To maintain a 20 percent share brand in Category A, on the other hand, you have to have 18 percent of the buyers buying both times, which is a 90 percent repeat rate. Anything less in this category will not yield a 20 percent share brand. By contrast, you would need only a 65 percent repeat rate to accomplish this share in Category E.

Looking at the average profitability in each of these categories (Exhibit 9), we see that its relative size is in direct proportion to that of the repeat rate required to maintain a given share.

To summarize, then, the repeat purchase rate for a product category—an analogue, as I mentioned before, for market concentration—offers a quick and easy way to screen potential new categories for their relative attractiveness for your company.

Because the repeat purchase rate is merely one way of expressing market concentration, these same profitability principles can be addressed for other categories—e.g., refrigerators—by employing other statistical expressions of concentration. We have demonstrated in packaged

Exhibit 8: Brand Repeat Purchase Slopes for Five Product Categories

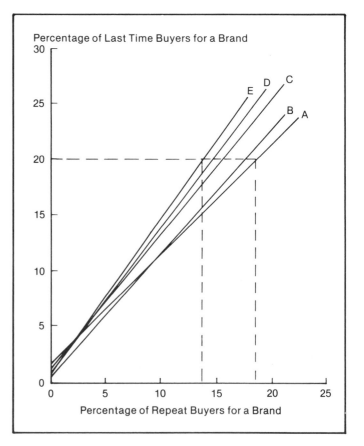

Exhibit 9: Brand Repeat Purchase Rates and Profitability for Five Product Categories

Product Category	20 Percent Share Brand Repeat Rate	Gross Trading Profit per $1.00 Sales
A............	90%	39.0¢
B............	85	29.3
C............	80	26.3
D............	75	25.3
E............	65	17.9

goods categories that both types of expressions correlate with profitability.

Substitutions

The issues of repeat purchase and of brand substitution are closely connected. The higher the repeat purchase rate, the less often the brand's customers substitute an alternative brand in that product category. Within a single category, one brand was found to get 40 percent of the category business from its own regular customers, while another brand, with comparable sales volume, got only 10 percent of its business this way.

As mentioned earlier, not all product categories fit neatly into groupings that permit the straight-forward analysis of repeat rates, either because the purchase cycle for the products is too long, or because it is not really possible to define the category (as, for example, when a product competes with things that appear markedly different from it). Increasingly, companies striving to avoid direct competition have marketed products within a relatively mixed competitive framework—so, often they can not meaningfully tell what their market share is. And they can not tell what the repeat purchase rate is, either.

Under these conditions what can be done, instead, is to employ another and actually more versatile type of measure. This is the measure of "substitutability." Such measurements can be made very easily through simple consumer surveys. The mechanics of such measurements are beyond the scope of my mission here, but product substitutability is not a difficult thing to establish.

Product substitutability measurements offer additional benefits for analysis. For one thing, you do not have to predetermine the competitive set of things that you are selling against—that is, the mixture of other brands and products with which your offering competes. For another, the substitution measure is not subject to short-term promotional manipulation (e.g., by marketing managers wishing to avoid control), as is the repeat rate. It is possible for someone who is trying to look good on repeat-rate numbers to introduce a price promotion into the market. And if research in that market is conducted in the brief period afterward, the subject brand's repeat-rate performance will look better than it ought to. Not

only is the substitutability measure not affected by such distortions, but it has been demonstrated that this measure also is directly reflective of the price elasticity of a product. It follows, therefore, that it is also correlated with the product's marketing profit potential.

To illustrate, Exhibit 10 charts the actual correlation for 25 different brands. The vertical scale represents the degree of substitutability, with low substitutability at the top and high substitutability at the bottom. The horizontal scale represents the manufacturer's net profit margin. As shown, there is a very strong relationship between low substitutability and high profitability.

For the 25 individual brands on the chart, which happened to cross several categories, the correlation between the substitution rate and the net profit margin was + .73. If you were to compare entire categories, however, instead of a varied mix of brands like this, you would sometimes find correlations as high as + .92. So the relative substitution rate turns out to be a powerful gauge of the price elasticity and potential profitability of one category versus another, as well as of the brands within a category (including both your own and those of your competitors).

Market Dominance

In determining which of several possible product areas would be good opportunity areas for expansion, another consideration is that of market dominance. Take the situation described in Exhibit 11, where each of two hypothetical product categories—A and B—has ten

Exhibit 10: Degree of Substitutability and Manufacturer's Net Profit Margin, 25 Selected Brands

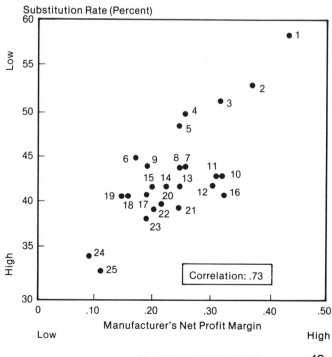

Exhibit 11: Relationship between Market Dominance and Additional Share Potential in Two Hypothetical Product Categories

Category	Share of Users—Ten Brands									
	1	2	3	4	5	6	7	8	9	10
A (percent)	50	30	10	3	2	1	1	1	1	1
B (percent)	35	20	8	6	6	5	5	5	5	5

Category	Average Share of Users
A (percent)	35
B (percent)	19

Category	Average Potential Share of an 11th Brand
A (percent)	26
B (percent)	16

brands. If you divide the 100 percent total brand share of the market that is possible by the total number of competing brands, you get in the case of each category a presumed average brand share of 10 percent. But a figure so computed is not a real average, and it could give misleading clues as to the effect of bringing a new brand into the picture.

What is needed is a weighted average, because some existing brands enjoy larger shares than others. Category A, in particular, is dominated heavily by a few brands. The weighted average brand share in Category A turns out to be 35 percent, and 19 percent in Category B. If you were to introduce an eleventh brand and did so on a parity basis—that is, with assurance of competitive product quality, distribution, pricing and everything else—you could then expect your most likely outcomes to be the generation of a 25 percent market share in Category A and a 16 percent share in Category B. This statistic is useful in assessing the relative cost of entry in alternative markets.

The Value of a Customer

Yet another factor in product appraisal is the value to the manufacturer of the brand's customers. The repeat-purchase customer for a brand, for example, has a measurable value to its manufacturer, which is the gross margin that the manufacturer is likely to earn from the customer in the course of a year. This important statistic for your brand determines how much you can afford to spend to acquire and hold a customer, an amount that differs by subgroups of products. Within a given category, customer value can also vary by brand, by geographic region, and so on.

Obviously, it can vary, too, by market segment—especially between heavy and light users—with the heavy user being the more valuable customer. The value of loyal users can be significant, even when they are light users of the product category; if you get 100 percent of their category business, they can be heavy brand users for you while remaining light category users. Such loyalty translates favorably into measures of the repeat purchase rate, substitutability, profitability, and the value of a customer. As for the value of purchases by product *triers,* which may be less than that for present customers, this varies greatly from category to category and also explains much of the difference in marketing behavior, such as the rate of new-product generation, between categories.

An actual analysis of the average value of a customer in each of ten product categories revealed a range from 48 cents to $42. Brands with the lowest values just cannot support advertising programs, because such brands cannot generate enough money to buy and hold a customer through advertising. Thus, it takes other kinds of marketing for the brand seller in such circumstances to be successful—the possibilities include the use of umbrella campaigns, divisional or corporate promotional identities, and the like, to support the brand.

At the other extreme are those cases where the value of a customer is so high that the company should arrange to market the brand all by itself, not as part of a line or a line extension. The company so blessed can well afford to develop a genuine consumer franchise for the product.

Knowledge of how much money is available for buying a customer affects the way the marketer might look at the marketing budget. As illustrated in Exhibit 12, one approach is to use the budget to sell the trade; while another approach is to use it to buy customers. The dollars can be the same in both cases, while the issue is viewed in two different ways. In the hypothetical case illustrated, the gross margin for your brand generates $100 million a year. Some 50 million cases of the item were sold to the trade, and 50 million cases were bought by consumers in the course of a year, with the case margin being $2.

When looking at your business with the trade—say, the grocery stores distributing the product—you can count 50,000 customers. But looking at your market the other way, you have 10 million consumers. In reviewing your marketing budget one way, you examine what you have to work with in selling the trade. Using your entire marketing budget in this way, the sum available to you is $2,000 per customer. Looking at the matter the other way, you have $10 to spend per consumer. If this is a new-product situation, what you have to decide is whether the venture will generate the dollars necessary to sell to the trade—and, alternatively, the dollars necessary to buy required numbers of consumers for the brand. In fact, you will always have to end up having to do each in some degree.

Exhibit 12: Assessing the Marketing Budget for a Hypothetical Brand Having a 10 Percent Share of Market

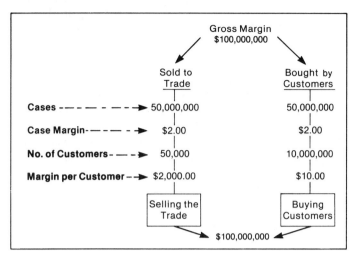

Screening Steps

All of the various measures I have described offer potential help to planners. In actually applying them in the screening of prospective product categories, my own preference is for a somewhat different order than presented here for discussion. A logical beginning is to look at share distributions first in the potential product categories to see which categories appear to be the most attractive from the standpoint of gain in a large—and, therefore, more profitable—market share. Then one can determine the value of a customer and multiply that value by the amount of volume the projected share implies. You may find that a product category that seemed more promising than another, because it offered a bigger market share, would, in fact, generate a smaller gross margin because the average value of a customer in that category is lower. If this value would not generate a large enough budget for the marketing job, then you can examine your second choice, perhaps trading off market dominance for the value-of-customer consideration, if this should prove to be necessary.

With no easy ways in the product category being considered to measure price elasticity directly, you can instead examine substitutability data for the category, as I have illustrated. Lastly, an analysis of the repeat purchase rate (or customer concentration) in the prospective category will tell you the rate you will need to maintain a given share level.

Trade-Offs for Established Products

Product substitutability, a particularly versatile measure, is useful not only in exploring new possibilities for the company. It can also be used in screening an existing product line to see which offerings should receive more support and which may be candidates for attrition or for conversion into regional brands.

Current brands can be assigned to four boxes, as shown in Exhibit 13, which classify them according to relative defensive and offensive strength. For gauging defensive strength, you can use the substitutability measure for your brands. Similarly, to classify your brands on the basis of their offensive strength, you can again refer to the substitutability of the other products in the category against which they are competing. If the substitutability for competing brands is higher than for yours, then your offensive strength is lower. If their substitutability is lower, then the offensive strength of your brand is higher and the competing items are more vulnerable. Opportunity Markets wind up in the upper-left box (Box 1) where both the defensive strength and offensive strength of your brands are high. In a Dormant Market (Exhibit 13, Box 2), your present franchise may be well protected. Your brand's defensive strength is high, but so is that of all the competing brands. Competition is slow as a result; and it matters little that your offensive strength may be low. Not much is going to be happening in the market, and your dollars would work inefficiently at trying to change people's purchase habits.

Box 3 represents a Volatile Market. You are relatively weak with your current customers, who are responsive to competitive inducements. Similarly, however, you are able to encroach on competitors' franchises with relative ease. Volatile markets exhibit heavy price and promotional competition, and it is wise to study means of shifting products from this market condition to one of higher defensive strength—even at the price of market share loss.

Exhibit 13: Marketing Allocation Segments

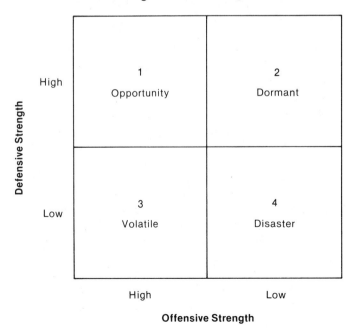

Exhibit 14: Marketing Allocation Segments for Equilibrium Strategy, Current Brands

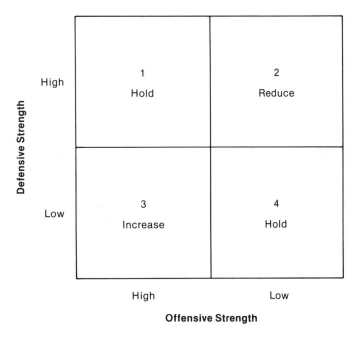

Exhibit 15: Marketing Allocation Segments for Polar Strategy, Current Brands

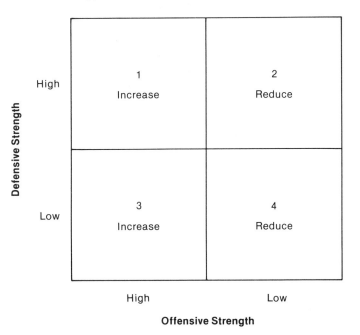

For brands in the fourth box, where your defensive strength is low and your offensive strength is also low, you are unlikely to survive. It is a Disaster Market.

In reality, of course, some managements are willing to take more risks than others. But assuming that the marketing budget is constant, the actions suggested in the four boxes of Exhibit 14 represent an "equilibrium strategy"—that is, a low-risk strategy that will not upset things in the market too much.

You might consider shifting some dollars out of brands in the dormant box toward those in the volatile box; and you might consider leaving brands in the other two boxes alone. That will be a low-risk strategy. You will seek to protect yourself in the volatile box, and business losses will be least likely in the dormant box where no one's marketing dollars are apt to produce much response.

A higher risk strategy is the "polar strategy" charted in Exhibit 15. Here you would not only shift marketing dollars out of the dormant box (Box 2) into the volatile box, but you would also shift dollars out of the vulnerable box into the opportunity box. This means that some of your brands very likely are going to die, but you have a continuing process for increasing your investment in winners and letting the losers wither by the wayside. The result will be to keep your product line profitable as the years go by.

The strategic consideration of offensive and defensive elasticity bears a surface similarity to the experience curve model because of the 2x2 matrix employed for simplifica-

tion. These two models, however, are quite different and often lead to conflicting directions which must be resolved in terms of the relative profit arising from production cost dynamics compared with that arising from marketing processes.

The experience curve model is predicated on an extension of the more familiar economic process whereby marginal-unit profitability rises with increasing utilization of productive capacity. Marketing processes are widely recognized as contributing to increased production profitability by producing increased sales—which translate into greater capacity utilization.

Not widely recognized, however, is the fact that marketing processes contribute to marginal profitability by a second process entirely unrelated to production cost efficiency. By various modes of communication, employing symbols of every sort—product features and cues; package design; advertising in words, pictures and sound; the use and nonuse of price promotion; the ratio of missionary sales to customer service; demonstration; the selection of distribution channels; and every means of brand and product differentiation—marketing alters the offensive and defensive elasticities of the product.

Often, in this manner, it is found that marginal marketing costs can be reduced relative to selling price by means which decrease relative sales, raising marginal production costs. This is the point at which we must speak separately of production profitability and of marketing profitability. Which choice to make in any concrete instance is a function of the relative effects of production profitability and of marketing profitability on the total profitability of the product.

And the decision does not rest there: Marketing may discover other consumption markets for which to design new products to employ the idle capital—thus increasing overall company profitability—even under conditions of reduced total profitability for the original product.

By combining the considerations of the production model (experience curve) with the considerations of the marketing model, we have the Compound Strategic Model.[1] Instead of a 4-cell (2x2) planning matrix, we now have a 16-cell model—with the greater diagnostic and planning flexibility it affords.

The Compound Strategic Model prescribes not only the quantitative allocation of resources between profit centers but also the qualitative allocation of resources between functional activities. In this manner, the Compound Strategic Model points out the means by which the market dynamics of a product may be altered so that they shift from a less profitable cell to a more profitable one.

[1] ©1980 Moran, Inc.

Part III

Formulating Strategy for the Industrial Product Line

Market Leverage

John L. Forbis
Principal
McKinsey & Company

AMONG THE COMPETITIVE strategy systems now evolving, some forms focus anew on the customer. Of course, they borrow heavily from prior marketing thinking, but their most important feature is their stress on a direct linkage between strategic thinking and the company's customers. The aim in doing so is to make the business significantly more profitable.

The primary question facing most business strategists, including most marketing people and those manning corporate technology departments, is how to create significant value faster than the competition—and thereby begin to achieve what might be called an "unfair" advantage for their companies. A second and related question is how to take that created value and share it with the customer in order to create significantly higher profits.

The corporate manager's primary concern these days, therefore, is not likely to be how to allocate scarce funds among two or three different businesses. Rather, it is likely to be how one might take these businesses and begin to create significantly higher profits from "unfair" advantages, making it possible, for example, to convert what may on the surface appear to be a "dog" business into a real "star."

The two axes of Exhibit 1 define two things managers should worry about when competing. The horizontal possibilities range from continuing in the same game to changing to a new game. The hypothesis, demonstrated in a number of cases, is that a company's ability to change the game to its advantage can, in fact, be a significant strength in deriving profits. In other words, if you are competing in a business where your competitors define the game, the chances are that they can actually set your rate of profit. On the other hand, if you can change the game to your advantage, perhaps through segmentation to get a stronger fix on the customer, you can probably end up with much higher profits.

A company's possibility at one extreme, as on the vertical scale of Exhibit 1, is to compete head-on. At the other end, it is to avoid competition. It is more fun to minimize or to avoid competition while supplying significant value to customers than to have to fight it out for sales all the way.

Too many of us are building strategies with businesses that are defined in the upper right-hand corner of the chart. We are competing head-on, and trying to play the same old game. Increasingly, smart managements are attempting to shift instead from same-game, head-on competition to new games and to greater avoidance of competition.

Naturally, there are many things affecting the possibilities and outcome—a company's cost position, its relative technical position, and so on. In approaching the question, there is merit in looking at our businesses from

Exhibit 1: Strategy Synthesis—"What Game to Play and How to Compete?"

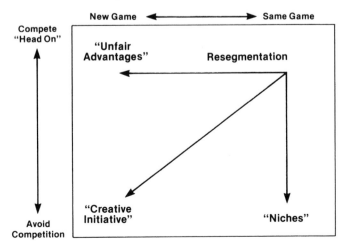

Exhibit 2: Illustration of Economic Value to the Customer

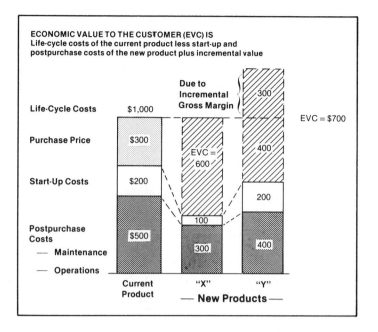

ECONOMIC VALUE TO THE CUSTOMER (EVC) IS
Life-cycle costs of the current product less start-up and
postpurchase costs of the new product plus incremental value

a customer's viewpoint, taking into account the concept that is sometimes called "economic value" to the customer. We must link strategic thinking to such considerations as internal costs, relative R and D capability, and the like. But, ultimately, it is the economic value that we can deliver to the customer—and our ability to differentiate it from our competitor's offering—that promises us maximum leverage in terms of profitability.

Economic Value to the Customer (EVC): An Example

This is not necessarily a new or revolutionary idea. But it is being applied nowadays in more practical ways than ever before. As illustrated in the left-most bar of Exhibit 2, the current cost to a customer for an existing industrial or engineered product is equal to the sum of the purchase price, the start-up costs, and the postpurchase costs for maintenance and operations. Proposed new product X, represented by the middle bar, would have a purchase cost of only $300 over the life of the product (as opposed to $500 for the existing product). And the installation cost for X, instead of being $200, would only be $100. The key point in this situation is that, relative to the life-cycle cost, the potential economic value to the customer is $500. In other words, the customer should be willing to pay up to $600 as the total purchase price for the new product—if, in fact, the kind of substitute situation described occurs.

Further, as the seller you may actually intend to provide the customer with some additional "noncost" or revenue features on that proposed product. (Possibly you are offering a telephone with new call-forwarding or dial-

ing features; or a computer with a higher rate of throughput; or a retail terminal that, because it allows additional billing information to be captured, can boost revenues and reduce losses.) If so, you have valuable leverage—not only in terms of the customer's cost outlay, but also in terms of other incremental revenue or margin being made available to the customer. Assume that the latter is valued at $300; then the ultimate Y product offered could be priced at $700.

Suppose the situation were somewhat different, and that you were in a market where you sold essentially on price. In this case, you could only charge a maximum of $300 for product Y. But consider, on the other hand, what would happen if you were to sell it on the basis of installed life-cycle cost. That would mean that the product could sell instead for about $600. And if you were able to convince the customer to buy product Y on the basis of the revenue impact, as well as of the cost impact, that would leave a potential EVC of $700. Therein lies an important concept for businesses that are experiencing slow growth: Consider expanding the value of your products to your customers, thereby giving you a greater margin to raise prices and significantly increase the sales base of one business compared with another.

Exhibit 3 offers an internal perspective on the business. Here the economic value is about $600, as it was for product X. In setting the price, the company can begin to weigh how much margin it wants to give the customer, and how much it wants to save as profit. A further extension of this concept can be the designing of products that actually allow us to differentiate our offerings from those of our competition and, thus, to sustain high rates of economic value.

Exhibit 3: Illustration of Customer Savings in EVC Context

EVC = $600

Customer Savings   200

Purchase Price
$400

Supplier's Profit   150

Supplier's Cost   250

"X"

* Customer savings is defined as EVC less the product price

Exhibit 4: Leverage from EVC Increase

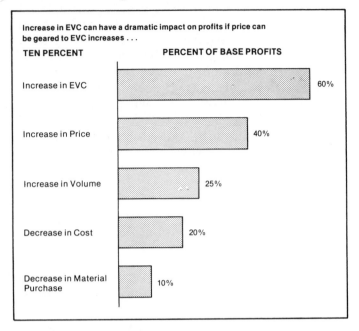

Increase in EVC can have a dramatic impact on profits if price can be geared to EVC increases . . .

TEN PERCENT	PERCENT OF BASE PROFITS
Increase in EVC	60%
Increase in Price	40%
Increase in Volume	25%
Decrease in Cost	20%
Decrease in Material Purchase	10%

Leverage through EVC

One merit of applying this concept of economic value to the customer (EVC), along with the simple kinds of sensitivity analysis that it permits, is that doing it so often points up a very useful fact: There can be more leverage on profits through increasing EVC than through increasing price, or increasing volume, or decreasing cost, or decreasing material price. (See Exhibit 4.)

The way to begin is by defining a business in terms of its economic value to the customer. Then, if possible, you convince the customer to buy on that basis. Through other strategy refinements, including the targeting of your R and D effort to enhance the inherent economic value offered and "managing" the price loss, you are more likely to get a lot more leverage out of the separate efforts of your various functional departments. This pragmatic approach offers opportunities for studying price, installation costs, postpurchase costs, and other elements to gauge the ultimate impact on the revenue of the customer. Armed with such information, it is possible to begin to think about how to serve one kind of customer compared with another. Maybe you should give special emphasis to that set of prospects and customers for which economic value is the greatest.

Segmenting Markets

Some promising uses of the EVC approach lie in segmenting markets, developing undivided product lines, focusing sales efforts and sales messages, and establishing strategic priorities. It may be best used in reviewing a market, a set of products, or an entire business in the company.

For starters, it is necessary to understand the customer base, including whatever broad variances may exist with respect to the intensity of product usage; geography; growth potential; and, finally, application. Many of these factors relate directly to the varying economic concerns of different types of customers. With improved insight into these concerns, we are in a better position to begin tailoring to advantage the product development efforts, sales efforts, or sales messages for the different user situations we have identified. Instead of emphasizing internal cost or price considerations throughout in building strategy, we can follow some basic notions that go back to the 1960's and 1970's focusing on the value of the product to the customer.

A manufacturer of turbine generators found EVC useful in resolving its pricing problems. The company served four principal segments, which differed mainly in their requirements of measured turbine output. The management was able to define the economic value for each segment, and it then reviewed the situation in light of the company's prevailing prices. The management quickly recognized the likely presence of a serious problem in one segment, which was confirmed in customer interviews. The exercise enabled it to weigh and to clarify its various options: Do we drop our price across the entire line? Do we begin to develop specialized products to focus on the problem segment? Do we segment our product line differently in order to combine two related segments to be served by one product, which would then give us some cost advantages? In actuality, the management was able to come up with a combined product-development and pricing strategy that would effectively maximize the company's profits.

One other thing the management learned in this review was that the economic value to customers in one segment was far above the price the company was charging. Thus, it was able to raise the price significantly in that segment, more than paying for the incremental development costs required to sustain a growth effort in the other segment. All in all, the manufacturer had gained information useful not only for short-term pricing, but also for guiding the firm's long-term development. (The same kinds of insights have come to others in the consumer products field—within such diverse areas as calculators and food processors.)

New Insights

Economic value analyses can be especially illuminating to the manager confronting a slow-growth environment. As unit volume began to taper off, one company began searching for ways to expand the value of its prime product to its customers. In the long run, it proved possible to keep sales volume growing through gradual, planned increases in that product's economic value. And so, instead of backing out of the business, or reducing its resources in the face of adversity, the company actually increased its resources to expand the economic value offered, thereby maintaining a dominant position of growth.

By putting the most talented people to work on the problem, the chances are good for finding and exploiting hidden values in ways that can reduce the need for competing on a same-game, head-on basis. The experience of a number of companies in diverse industries suggests that a strategy emphasizing value to the customer, and not the company's own costs, can lead to significantly greater profits.

Optimal Breadth and Depth of the Line

John W. Peterson
Divisional Vice President
  and General Manager
Diamond Products Division
Norton Company

IN SETTING STRATEGY, the manufacturer of industrial products must decide on the optimum breadth and depth of the company's product line. Partly, it is the equivalent question to that of Heinz: Should we have 56 or 58 varieties instead of 57?

To clarify in a rather arbitrary way what is *breadth* and what is *depth* in a product line, I would like to propose some definitions. First, for product line *breadth,* related product types are at issue. That is, if you are in the valve business, your potential product types might be ball valves and slide valves. If you are in the automobile business, your product types might be full-sized cars and compact cars. If you are in the abrasives business, your product types might be coated abrasives and grinding wheels. In each case, there is a reasonably close relationship—with respect to raw material, manufacturing process, distribution channel or end user—that ties these product types together.

The idea of *depth,* however, suggests product variations. For instance, within your ball-valve product type, possible variations offered might include manual valves and automatic valves. Within the full-sized car type, variations might include two-door models, four-door models, and so forth. Grinding wheel variations might include vitrified-bonded wheels and resin-bonded wheels.

Pressures on the Marketer

With these definitions of "breadth" and "depth" in mind, how do we marketers go about identifying the *optimum* product types and product variations to offer to the marketplace? This is not an idle question to be debated over cocktails and sales meetings and forgotten until next year, because as marketing managers we are often and actively challenged to make changes in our company's product offering.

- Who in the industrial field has not had an irate customer demand that a specialty be added to the line—always to be sold at the commodity price?
- Who has not had the sales force demand several different price and quality levels to satisfy all the various customer demands?
- Who has not been pressed by manufacturing management to sell only the easy-to-make, long-run products—the kinds that make the factory numbers look good?
- Who has not listened to the controller explain the need to sell the profitable products and to eliminate the marginal ones—even though the products may be interdependent in the marketplace?
- Who has not listened to a distributor insist that the company's product line must be just as broad as those of competitors?

How are we to respond to these well-intentioned and often emotional pleas to change the types or the variations of our product offerings? There are many management approaches to the problem. And I would not suggest that the strategy-based approach which I strongly prefer is the only valid solution.

For instance, it is very tempting to examine each proposal for change in product type or product variation for its effect on long-term profitability:

- How would the change affect sales?
- How would sales of other products in the line be affected?
- How would competitors respond?
- How would the change be received by distributors?
- How would prices be affected?

- How would material and manufacturing costs be affected?
- How would selling and administrative costs be affected?

The interrelationships raised by these questions are often quite complex. And it is always possible that, while a decision based on answers to these questions is right for the specific proposal, it is wrong for the overall business.

The Strategy-Based Approach

For this reason, my preference is for a broader framework, one that provides general guidance both for responding to the demands for product-line change and for future product-line planning. Such an approach (1) defines a "business," and then (2) defines a strategy for this business. Once these definitions are in hand, it becomes far easier to make product-line decisions that are consistent, rather than at odds, with the strategy.

A business is some grouping of products, competitors, distributors and/or customers that can stand more or less on its own. Changes in products, prices and service in this particular business will have little ripple effect on other businesses within the corporation. Defining a business is not easy and is rarely clear-cut, but we do break down our corporations into more manageable pieces as a natural and normal thing. If a business can stand on its own, then it is possible to identify a separate strategy for the business that may be different from the strategies for other businesses in the corporation.

With a relatively free-standing business and a strategy settled upon, we have the framework to identify an appropriate product-line strategy. I will attempt to define five common successful strategies and then suggest some product-type and product-variation guidelines that are appropriate to these strategies. Briefly, they are:
(1) Exploit a proprietary product or process.
(2) Maintain or expand a large market share.
(3) Exploit a scarce or unique resource.
(4) Identify a defensible subsegment and maintain or expand a large market share in the subsegment.
(5) Use a Number 2 position to advantage.

Taking these one at a time, let us see what product-line decisions make sense.

The Proprietary Product

The proprietary product is almost a classic in appropriate product-type and product-variety decisions. What is the objective of a patent-based strategy? Simple! Do everything necessary so that when the patent protection is eroded, the patent holder has the large market share necessary to executive strategy number 2—i.e., maintaining or expanding that share.

What does this imply? First, it is important to get down the learning curve with the basic invention. Second, it is important to have all the major end uses for the invention covered when the patent runs out. So, if the strategy is to run fast with a proprietary product or process, an optimum product strategy would seem to be:
(1) Expand the number of product types.
(2) Keep product variations to a minimum.

Executed well, this strategy is awesome. In one case I am familiar with, a company patented a material with possible commercial, industrial and consumer uses. Recognizing the commercial use as offering the largest short-term volume, the company first pushed this market hard, to get down the manufacturing learning curve. Product variations were kept to an absolute minimum. Then, in an orderly fashion, industrial and, finally, consumer product types were introduced.

As time wore on, a very few variations were provided to the marketplace years later. By the time litigation had proven the patent invalid, the only market opportunities left to competitors were in minor variations. All of the center ground of all markets had been preempted; the company could easily respond to any new wrinkles introduced by others; and its cost position was invincible.

Maintaining or Expanding a Large Share

The second possible strategy is to maintain or expand a large *market share.* The objective, of course, is to capitalize on a wide variety of economy-of-scale opportunities. Many major costs are more costly per unit of sales to the smaller market-share holder than to the large market-share holder. One only needs to view the current GM-Chrysler positions in regard to development of economical cars to recognize how powerful this strategy is.

What product-type and variation guidelines are appropriate to the large-share strategy? Here are some possibilities:
(1) Cover the business marketplace with the necessary product types. Again, the famous GM principle of segmenting the car market and providing a product type appropriate to each segment is well-known.
(2) Keep new or advanced products coming.
(3) Keep variations from becoming extreme. That is, leave the small fringe areas of questionable profitability to small competitors.
(4) Seek commonality between types and variations, if at all possible, to obtain obvious manufacturing economies.
(5) Eliminate obsolete or small specialty products from the line.

The tough question to be answered most often by the large-share holder is this: Is the product type or variation being advocated a fringe specialty that would best be avoided; or does it represent a growing market that is destined for a big future and must not be passed up? The reluctance of a large-share holder to make a change because of negative implications to economies of scale can lead to trouble. If a factory is all tooled up to make an inch-dimensioned product, it can be hard to duplicate the tooling in metrics.

Getting rid of small, unprofitable specialties is easier said than done. The philosophy in our company is to avoid leaving a customer in the lurch by abruptly discontinuing a product variation. But, as Peter Drucker urges: "Make sure you get paid for specialties." So we gradually raise prices to slowly dry up demand for the variation. As prices rise, the net effect in more than a few cases is not to shift customers to alternate sources of supply but, rather, to turn marginal specialties into worthwhile profit generators.

Exploiting the Scarce Resource

The third possible strategy is to exploit a scarce resource. We are all familiar with the Monopoly game; and very early we learned that you could do a lot if you owned both the Boardwalk and Park Place. While there are very few OPEC's or Bell Systems around, there are other opportunities for exploiting restricted or scarce resources. Key scientists may be in very short supply; high-grade raw material sources may be few in number; or good distribution channels in a market may be scarce. In markets outside of the United States, protection can sometimes be obtained for a domestic producer there.

What product-line strategy is optimum for the business capitalizing on a scarce resource? A suggested guideline is that the product types and variations must be adequate to keep the semimonopoly whole. As an example, if Bell has only leased phones available—and there is a demand for phones to be purchased outright—part of the monopoly can be broken. If good distributors are few and far between, then the product types and variations offered must be wide enough to avoid loss of these scarce distributors to competitors who offer a more satisfactory product mix. If the host country feels that a domestic producer is not satisfying the majority of the country's needs, the result could well be a second domestic competitor.

Incidentally, our experience has been that considerable attention must be paid to the stage of industrialization of emerging foreign markets. Assuming that the appropriate U.S. product types and variations are appropriate in an emerging country can lead to unpleasant consequences. Frequently, the right move is to wind back the hands of time in the product-life cycle, and to provide a simpler, less specialized product line in the emerging market.

The Defensible Subsegment

The fourth possible strategy—the defensible subsegment—can be based on a product, a distribution channel, or a market. The objective of this strategy, of course, is to identify a product, channel or market that is small enough in size so that the large-share holder, with a very broad product line, will yield rather than fight in this small specialty area. Once the segment is identified, then the strategy objective is to become good enough in that area to enjoy the advantages of having a large share (that is, the economies of scale) in a very narrow segment.

For the defensible subsegment, the suggested optimal situation is: (1) there should probably be only one product type; (2) within this type the variations should cover the target product, channel or market like a blanket; and (3) the company should maintain product or process innovations. In almost any industry, there can be found a narrow-line specialist who does very well by following these suggestions.

The Compatible Number 2

The last strategy could be called "the compatible Number 2." The idea is to make acceptable returns by coexisting with competitor Number 1—the largest share holder. Confrontation must be avoided, because in an all-out struggle Number 2 would surely lose. Again, the highly visible automotive example suggests that GM will allow Ford to make *satisfactory* returns as long as GM can make *superior* returns.

In general, Number 2 will be saying to its customers or distributors: "Our product is just as good as Number 1's, but our price is a little lower." If price and product were equal, the business would probably go to Number 1.

How is Number 2 able to get satisfactory returns despite the price disadvantage? Certainly, product-line policy is one of the few weapons available to Number 2. Customers and distributors expect somewhat less from Number 2—even though they will never admit it. If Number 2 is astute enough to identify the marginal specialties into which Number 1 is trapped and to steer clear of these, it can help its situation.

So, the product-type and variation guideline for Number 2 must be, first, to identify Number 1's marginal losers and, second, to avoid them like the plague. Turn a deaf ear on all the pressure that says Number 2 must meet Number 1 head-on in all markets, in all channels, and in all products.

Summary

We have seen that for each of five potentially successful strategies, certain product-type and product-variation guidelines seem to make sense. Summarizing those strategy-based approaches to optimum product-line breadth and depth:

- We can define "breadth" as product type.
- We can define "depth" as variations of this basic product type.
- To identify the optimum product types and variations, it is important to have a logical structure

and then to make decisions that are consistent with this structure. A strategy-based approach is one way to do this.

- The suggested structure is, first, to identify a "business"—a comfortable group of products channels, competitors and customers than can stand pretty much alone.
- The second part of the structure is to identify a strategy for each "business."
- For each business and intended strategy, product-type and variation decisions can be made that are consistent with the key objectives of the strategy.
- Five possible strategies, along with a consistent product-line approach for each, have been suggested.

I make no claim that the strategy-based approach cited will cover all of the optimal decisions on product-line breadth and depth that may arise. But such an approach can help you to avoid major errors—decisions that are inconsistent with an appropriate business strategy.

Identifying New Competitive Opportunities

Bruce J. Hoesman[1]
Vice President—Planning
  and Business Development
American Hospital Supply Corporation

PLANNING IS A CIRCULAR PROCESS within a company, requiring automatic feedbacks and continuing adjustments and improvements. In the case of our company, for example, the environment for planning is affected by our customers, by our competitors, by the economy, and by government and regulatory factors that have a heavy impact on health care.

One important element of planning for the American Hospital Supply Corporation relates to the development of business. In support of that planning, we make use of a proactive mechanism for identifying new opportunities for competitive action—such as the entering of new markets or the launching and marketing of new product lines.

That mechanism has become an important part of our strategic planning process, which has a three-to-five year horizon. The results, linked to our strategies for the remainder of our business, help to shape our capital plans for plants, machinery and equipment in coming years, and also our shorter term operating plans. In our scheme of things, operating planning has a one-to-three year horizon, and this is where we make our strategic plans come to life.

At American Hospital Supply, we plan by market segment. We do not plan the $2.5 billion corporation from the top down. Rather, we plan from the bottom up, one market segment or product line at a time. That goes for every element of the process—including plans for new business development, strategy, capital spending, and operations.

We have used—and still use—a variety of planning tools and approaches, including PIMS (Profit Impact of

[1]Now Executive Vice President of Abbey Medical/Abbey Rents, Inc., a wholly owned subsidiary of American Hospital Supply Corporation.

Market Strategy) and portfolio analysis. At best, most fill in only part of the picture. One difficulty with portfolio analysis, for example, is that it is "today oriented." It can become the basis for strategic planning, but it will not necessarily lead you to identify and capitalize on competitive opportunities. For our special needs we drew, in part, on some of these other approaches to design our planning system for new business development. Although it is tailored to our business, it is likely that most of its elements will find application in your business, too.

Our system is designed to give us a way to evaluate the likely success of products, market entries, acquisition candidates, research and development projects. The model recognizes the real importance of synergy (an often used word that is rarely used correctly). I learned very early in my career that if all you can bring to the party in a business opportunity is money—and not sales, manufacturing or technical strengths—you should not come to the party at all: You are behind to begin with, and you will have to build all the strengths that are necessary to compete.

Elements of the Model

In its barest essentials, our new business development model is composed of 20 major factors, with some 140 subfactors. Each major factor—say, our company's relative market share—is weighted high, medium or low, based upon its impact on the business, which is judgmental. The model is broken down into two major components: (1) external and market factors, and (2) internal and profitability factors.

For our purposes, we isolate 11 external and market factors. (Other businesses might choose more or fewer.) The first five listed in Exhibit 1 are all considered to be high-impact factors deserving the maximum potential of

Exhibit 1: External and Market Factors

- Total market dollars
- Market growth rate
- Market share
- Relative growth rate
- Relative market share
- Market concentration
- Product characteristics
- Buying influences
- Extent of government involvement
- Defensive aspects
- Future considerations

Exhibit 2: Internal and Profitability Factors

- Gross profitability
- Net earnings after tax
- Return on net working assets
- Cash flow
- Strength of manufacturing
- Strength of distribution
- Strength of sales force
- Strength of R and D and product development
- Strength of market communications

12 points each. Take, for example, total market dollars—that is, the total market potential. In our scheme of things, to get twelve points for that, the market must exceed $20 million. If it is between $10 and $19 million, the opportunity rates eight points; $5 to $9 million is worth four points; and any market below $4 million is weighed as zero. In another company, the appropriate comparable criteria would depend upon the specific market dynamics and the markets it serves.

As for the market growth-rate factor, I should point out that in the health-care industry, we are unusually blessed because we do have some very robust markets, including areas of potentially high technology and/or rapid conversion. In our scheme of things, if the market is growing at 20 percent or more each year, we assign it a value of 12 points. Between 17 and 19 percent the value is eight points; for 15 or 16 percent it is four; and below 14 percent it is zero.

Market share is, of course, a relatively straightforward concept; but the relative growth-rate factor, as we consider it, may deserve some explanation. Although it is very similar to relative market share, it represents, instead, the expected growth rate in the company's sales versus the growth rate for the market as a whole. For instance, if a market is growing at 10 percent, and you believe that your company's sales within it can grow at 15 percent, that is a 1.5 relative growth rate. If you believe that your sales can grow at 20 percent in a market growing at 10 percent, that is a 2.0 relative growth rate. So anytime that your relative growth rate is over 1.0, you are, in fact, "oversharing" or gaining in market share.

In our scheme, if the relative growth rate is 1.5 or better, the market opportunity warrants 12 points. If it is 1.2 to 1.4, it is worth eight points. At 1.0, we assign it four points. If we were evaluating the prospects in other industries, our criteria might well be different, but the general principle would still apply.

Among the other six external and market factors, I might mention that for one of them—product characteristics—the question is how much opportunity we have to innovate and to clearly differentiate product

features and benefits. If the answer is a lot, then the maximum score is given. Where the features are somewhat—if not clearly—differentiable, only a medium point-score is assigned; and "me-too's" simply get zero.

Not all of the factors considered carry a maximum weight of 12 for us. For example, that for "buying influences" is six. In our business, if the buyer is a medical practitioner—that is, a doctor or a nurse supervisor who makes the purchase decision based upon product merits—the full six points are awarded. If the buying influence is a mixture of medical practitioners and support personnel, this calls for four points. And when the total buying decision is done by strictly supporting personnel, such as the purchasing agent, and without consultation with a medical practitioner, that is worth two points.

Once each of the external factors is rated, we simply add up the total. In our case, the potential aggregate points come to 97. Recently, one opportunity being reviewed received 89 points out of the possible 97. Thus, its total ranking was 92 percent, suggesting a very attractive area. Another was only 67 percent, which is not so good. We have chosen to use 80 percent as a breakpoint, and have elected not to pursue anything that ranks below that.

In the other section dealing with internal and profitability factors (Exhibit 2), the first four deal specifically with profitability. Expected gross margin, for example, counts for a lot, as does net earnings potential. Both are expressed as a percent of sales and not necessarily a reflection of absolute dollars. Return on net working assets is also rated high, with a 12-point potential. In our system, any opportunity having a five-year pro forma return on net working assets of 25 percent or more gets 12 points. Between 20 and 24 percent, it rates eight points; 17 to 19 percent, four points; and zero points below 17 percent. With the present cost of capital, these numbers are being raised.

Cash flow is also important to our business, particularly when interest rates are high. Opportunities that can generate a net inflow of funds in three of the next five years get maximum points. With such inflow in one or two of the five years, medium points are assigned; and a break-even situation gets the lowest grade.

In the next group of internal and profitability factors, we count on synergy. That indicates what you can bring to the party—whether it is an acquisition, a joint venture, or a new-product opportunity. For the most part, we rank these all the same way and require sound judgment in rating them. In general, when a new product under consideration strongly capitalizes on strengths we already have—in manufacturing, distribution, sales, research and development, or promotion—it deserves a maximum score in each of these categories. If some strengths need to be augmented, they may get medium points, with each rated separately. If we lack the necessary strength, we rate it low and count on no synergy. In these cases, we are probably in a situation where we can bring nothing to the party except money—and anyone can do that!

Once again, after each of the internal and profitability factors has been ranked, we add up the potential, just as we do with the external factors. In our case, the total possible is 96 points. So, if a rating is 85 out of 96 (89 percent), we will go for the venture. If it is only 70 out of 96 (73 percent), we keep looking.

In our experience, a rating system like this offers an objective and systematic starting point for appraising new ventures and formulating growth strategy. We also believe that there are advantages to establishing a working group to gain action—what we call our new business development committee. Such a committee should cut across functional lines, with members comprised of the top executive in each discipline—marketing, sales, manufacturing, research and development, personnel and others.

It is important, too, to establish a mechanism for identifying opportunities. And for this, you really want to rely on each committee participant to provide a perspective from his or her vantage point in the business.

When the committee uses our rating systems to evaluate proposed ventures, the results can be surprising. The members have to be objective and not try to fool the system because, if they do, it will send them along the wrong path. Usually, the committee rates the first few opportunities as a group. Next, they discuss each specific factor and make their ratings. The committee then ranks the projects from top to bottom and subjects them to an established cutoff point, usually 80 percent. They then focus on the top three or four projects, analyze them in detail, and select the one or two having the highest probability for success.

The Results

Does this approach work? For us it has. In one market segment, for instance, we launched an internal venture with two acquisitions and one joint venture. That market segment now has a 30 + percent growth rate and profitability to match. Why? Because there was good, sound planning, an identification of opportunities, and, most important, plenty of synergy at work.

In another segment, the acquisition route was blocked and so we opted for a 100 percent internal development program—relying on our own research and development and building a new venture. This effort is beginning to come to fruition with some innovative products, some market leadership products, along with some "me-too" items.

Have we had failures? None since adopting this system, although before that we did. Nowadays we are very selective in what we pursue. As we expand we may well have some failures, because, after all, business entails risk. The key is to know when to take risks and when not to. A systematic approach to the problem surely makes that decision a lot easier.

Pricing New Industrial Products

Kent B. Monroe[1]
Head, Department of Marketing
Virginia Polytechnic Institute
  and State University

AMERICAN BUSINESS has been criticized for being too "risk aversive." That is, companies seemingly have been unable to venture into new products, new markets, or new strategies without the prior probabilities of success being relatively high. Despite a marketing environment vastly different from previous ones, they have been generally slow to recognize that the old way of pricing products and services must be reanalyzed and, often, changed. In addition, only recently have some industrial products firms recognized and begun to use the results from pricing research conducted in this country and abroad. Being risk-aversive, they have rarely attempted pricing that is not mainly cost-based. Today, however, a number of such firms are successfully employing an approach that explicitly recognizes demand to be the key to profitable pricing decisions.

Factors to Consider

There are certain key factors to consider when setting price (Exhibit 1). Demand considerations provide a ceiling or maximum price that may be charged. The determination of this maximum price depends on the customers' perceptions of value in the seller's product/service offering. On the other hand, costs provide a floor, or minimum possible price. For existing products, the relevant costs are the direct costs associated with the production and marketing of these products. For a new product, the relevant costs are the future direct costs over that product's life cycle. Research and development costs are sunk, or past, costs that are not relevant to the new

[1]Portions of this chapter have been drawn by the author from his book, *Pricing: Making Profitable Decisions*. Copyright 1979 by McGraw-Hill, Inc. Used with permission of the author and McGraw-Hill Book Company.

Exhibit 1: Conceptual Orientation to Pricing

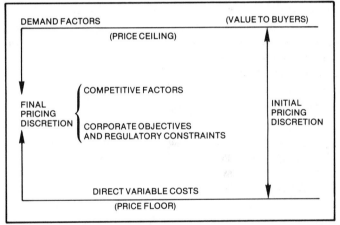

product pricing decision. As Exhibit 1 shows, the difference between what buyers are willing to pay (value) and the minimum, cost-based price represents an initial pricing discretion. However, this range of pricing discretion is narrowed by competitive factors, corporate profit and market objectives, and regulatory constraints. Primarily, competitive factors act to reduce the price ceiling, whereas corporate objectives and regulation act to raise the minimum possible price. The result is that final pricing discretion is limited to a more narrow, feasible range.

It is also important to note that loading irrelevant costs onto a new product's burden may simply push the price floor beyond the price ceiling, leading to a decision to set the product's price too high. Recently, a medical equipment producer, a supplies manufacturer, and an industrial machinery producer all experienced new product failures due to setting too high an introductory price. What is most critical of all when developing a new product's price is the relationship between buyers' perceived benefits in the new product relative to the total acquisition cost. One approach for assessing buyers' perceived value is to conduct a value analysis.

Value Analysis

A common fallacy associated with industrial pricing is the belief that the industrial buyer acts solely to minimize the price paid. Indeed, there is ample evidence that the industrial buyer, much like the consumer, tends to use price as an indicator of value. Thus, the low-price supplier does not often achieve a dominant market position. For example, in the agri-chemical industry, the lowest priced product in one product category had, over time, maintained a market share of 2 to 4 percent with no recent sales growth. However, the company substantially raised the product's price to be consistent with competitive offerings, with the result that sales are now growing steadily. The important thing is the ratio between benefits received (value) and the total cost of acquiring the product or service:

$$\frac{\text{Perceived}}{\text{Value}} = \frac{\text{Perceived Benefits}}{\text{Price}}$$

(Where price is the total cost to the buyer: purchase price + acquisition costs + transportation + installation + order handling + risk of failure; and perceived benefits are determined by physical attributes, service attributes and technical support available in relation to the particular use of the product.)

The research needed to determine the buyers' perceived value of an offering includes value analysis and value engineering. Value analysis attempts to determine the relative value (utility) that buyers place on the total product/service offering—that is, the perceived benefits. Value engineering attempts to determine methods of reducing the total cost without diminishing the delivered value.

To use value analysis and value engineering in pricing, it is useful to distinguish four components of perceived value:
(1) Cost—the sum of all costs required to produce and deliver the product;
(2) Exchange—the ability to obtain a certain price from the marketplace;
(3) Aesthetic—the value placed on the properties or attractiveness of the product;
(4) Relative use—for example, use value will increase with the life span of a machine, or with the reduction in fuel consumption.

The key to value analysis is to remember that the customer wants something done and he or she wants someone satisfied. Buyers want something enclosed, held, moved, separated, cleaned, heated, cooled, or whatever, under certain conditions and within certain limits; and/or they want a shape, a color, an aroma, a texture, a sound, a "precious" material, or whatever to bring satisfaction to themselves or to others they wish to please.

Current research evidence suggests that it is the buyer's perception of total relative value that provides the willingness to pay a particular price for a given offering. In any specific pricing situation, it is essential to find out what attributes of the offering are perceived as most important to the buyer. Then, either tradeoff analysis or possibly conjoint measurement may be used to determine the relative value of different attribute combinations. Finally, the research needs to determine the perceived performance of competitive offerings on the attributes identified as important.

As suggested above, value analysis concentrates on increasing perceived value by increasing performance relative to the customer's needs and willingness to pay for that performance. Value engineering, on the other hand, concentrates on increasing value by decreasing costs while maintaining performance. Generally, the importance of value engineering increases as the product moves through its life cycle. Particularly, as maturity is reached, efforts must be made to identify unnecessary costs and to arrange for their removal while maintaining performance levels.

A number of factors lead to the inclusion of unnecessary costs in a product. During the research and development stage, major efforts are devoted to providing a performance level that meets the customer's requirements. Often, deadlines are imposed that do not permit complete searching, testing, and obtaining information that would result in meeting the customer's needs at lowest cost. Similarly, the imposition of deadlines does not permit adequate attention to the purchasing, manufacturing, and marketing activities for the product.

A continuing flow of new ideas, processes, products and materials can help to establish and maintain product performance levels at lower cost. Through value engineering it is possible to incorporate more of this new information sooner and to minimize the product's advancement toward value obsolescence.

The key point is that the buyer will make a purchase decision on the basis of perceived value, not solely on the basis of minimizing the price paid. Moreover, the price set must be consistent with the value perception. That is, a product perceived to be of higher value than competitive offerings will be granted the privilege of a premium price.

Cost Analysis

"Cost is probably the least important of the considerations in . . . setting . . . product prices. . . . Costs can[not] be ignored in the establishment of pricing policies. . . . Distribution [and marketing] costs are of the same importance [in setting product prices] as are production or acquisition costs. The common practice of adding a percentage (usually of manufacturing cost) to cover selling and administrative expense is a wholly inadequate recognition of this fact."[2]

Perhaps the most common error companies make in pricing new products is to attempt to recover their investment in the new product as quickly as possible. A reasonable price for a new product is one that will attract both resellers and ultimate users. A high price requiring substantial selling effort to overcome buyer resistance will not receive enthusiastic support from distributors.

A second common error producers make in pricing new products is to base their initial prices on the wrong cost data. Including development costs and high initial unit production costs in the new product's costs will likely result in a price that will repel both distributors and final customers, and effectively kill the product. Development costs must be considered as an investment to be recovered over the life of the product. The appropriate unit direct costs are those costs expected when the product reaches its growth stage, or when steady production and sales rates are achieved. The value of the experience curve becomes readily apparent for forecasting these relevant direct costs.

It is important to remember that fixed costs occur because of a legal, contractual or moral obligation, and they are not caused by the depreciation of fixed assets or the write-off of developmental sunk costs. There are good reasons for charging depreciation, but the amount calculated is by some arbitrary formula and is not a relevant cost for pricing a new product. What is relevant is whether the development costs and investment in fixed assets are recovered over the life of the product. Do the returns from the sale of the product justify the investment?

Approaching Price Strategy

A major consideration for pricing new products is the recognition that the management of a multiproduct firm should be concerned with managing products over the products' life cycles. Therefore, it is imperative that the strategic plans consider the life cycles of sales, total contribution, separable fixed costs, and separable assets employed with the different products. Moreover, management must control production and marketing

[2]*Handbook of Modern Accounting,* 2nd ed. New York: McGraw-Hill, Inc. 1977, p. 43-10.

Exhibit 2: Investment Life Cycle

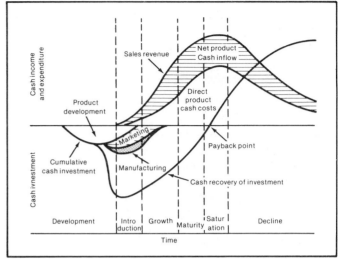

Source: Adapted from John Sizer, "Accountants, Product Managers and Selling Price Decisions in Multi-Consumer Product Firms," *Journal of Business Finances,* 4 (Spring 1972), 76.

costs as well as the level of common costs and common assets employed.

Indeed, the experience-curve evidence suggests that, as the product sales grow, costs and price decline. However, there is another common pricing fallacy which assumes that there are automatic cost reduction opportunities as accumulated volume grows. Although it is logical to expect unit cost reduction due to the learning curve, value engineering, and production process improvements, it is nevertheless true that these cost reductions are not automatic, nor are they generally available for each situation. Moreover, for a low-margin product, relatively large cost reductions are necessary before the experience factor is profitable. There is also a tendency for the level of common costs and common assets employed to increase with growth in product sales. Hence, uncontrolled growth in common costs can erode direct-cost reductions due to accumulated experience. Recently, I have worked with the managements of several industrial product companies who believed they operated on an experience curve but had absolutely no evidence of what their cost reductions were.

The intuitive appeal of the product life cycle, its theoretical foundation in the adoption process, and empirical verification suggest the model's validity. Yet there is no fixed time length for a cycle, nor for the lengths of the various stages within a life cycle. If anything, advancing technological growth has led to a shortening of the typical life cycles. And, as shown in Exhibit 2, the profitability life cycle is even shorter. Thus, managements need to recognize that:

(1) Products have limited life;
(2) Under accelerating technological growth, product life span is likely to be shorter than ever;
(3) Sales and profits tend to follow a predictable trend;

(4) Products require different marketing strategies at each stage of the life cycle;

(5) Pricing strategy is vitally important at each stage of the life cycle, but particularly so at the introduction stage.

Estimating Demand for a New Product

The first step in new product pricing is to estimate demand in the selected market targets. But how can demand for new products be estimated? How can the range of prices that buyers will consider acceptable for a new product which they have never seen or used be estimated?

This problem of demand estimation can be separated into a series of research problems. The first is concerned with whether the product itself will fill a need or want, and will therefore sell if the price is right. The second research problem is to determine the range of prices that will make the product economically acceptable to potential buyers. Then, expected sales volumes must be estimated at feasible price points in the acceptable price range. Finally, it is necessry to determine the potential competitive reaction.

Alternative Strategies

It has been generally presumed that there are two alternatives in pricing a new product. One is "skimming" pricing which calls for a relatively high price; and the other is "penetration" pricing, which calls for a relatively low price. A *skimming price* may be appropriate for new products if:

(1) Demand is likely to be price inelastic;

(2) There are likely to be different price-market segments, thereby appealing to those buyers first who have a higher range of acceptable prices;

(3) Little is known about the costs of producing and marketing the product;

(4) A capacity constraint exists;

(5) There is realistic value (perceived) in the product/service.

A *penetration price* may be appropriate if:

(1) Demand is likely to be price elastic in the target market segments;

(2) Competitors are expected to enter the market quickly;

(3) There are no distinct and separate price market segments;

(4) There is the possibility of large savings in production and marketing costs if a large sales volume can be generated (i.e., the experience factor).

Caution is suggested in any selection of either skimming or penetration pricing strategy. Generally, there is at least one currently existing product that will serve as a frame of reference to potential buyers and they are likely to use this product to form their opinons about the value and price of the new product. Where such a reference product exists, the price setter must determine the appropriate price differential (higher or lower price than the reference product) and fit the new product into the established population of existing products.

The factors just mentioned may suggest an overall pricing strategy for a new product. However, the two alternative strategies cited—skimming and penetration—should not be viewed as either/or alternatives. Rather, they merely reflect two opposite strategy extremes. Considerable latitude, therefore, exists in choosing the specific price level for a new product. Let us now turn to the problem of deciding on the actual price level for such a product.

Contribution Analysis

Ideally, the analysis and planning for pricing of a new product begins at the start of the product development stage. One primary consideration for accepting a new product proposal and initiating the developmental investment is the rate of return on investment expected during the product's life. But the investment analysis requires an estimate of revenues and expenditures over time for each alternative under consideration. And there is an explicit price-volume-cost relationship that influences both revenues and expenditures. As Exhibit 2 indicates, the analysis must project estimated cash flows over the entire investment life cycle. Therefore, it is necessary at the outset to have some preliminary price-volume estimates for the different stages of the product life cycle.

Much of the analysis relevant to the pricing of a new product involves contribution analyses. For clues to alternative, feasible prices and to expected, reasonable costs a profit-volume break-even chart can be constructed, as shown in Exhibit 3. (The data for this chart are shown in Table 1.) While the break-even chart reveals different break-even points for prices P_1 through P_6, it provides no information on price-demand-cost-profit relationships. It

Exhibit 3: Break-Even Chart: Price-Volume Combinations for New-Product Pricing

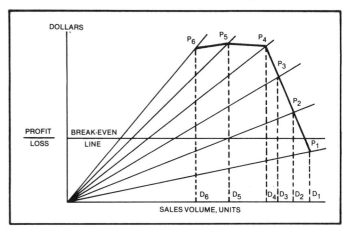

Table 1—Price-Volume Data for Life-Cycle Pricing at Introductory Stage

Unit Selling Price	$6.50	$7.00	$7.50	$8.00	$8.50	$9.00
Unit Variable Cost	6.00	6.00	6.00	6.00	6.00	6.00
Unit Contribution	$0.50	$1.00	$1.50	$2.00	$2.50	$3.00
PV (profit-volume-ratio)	0.077	0.143	0.200	0.250	0.294	0.333
Volume (units)	1,500,000	1,400,000	1,300,000	1,225,000	1,000,000	800,000
Revenue	$9,750,000	$9,800,000	$9,750,000	$9,800,000	$8,500,000	$7,200,000
Fixed Expenses	$1,000,000	$1,000,000	$1,000,000	$1,000,000	$1,000,000	$1,000,000
Variable Costs	$9,000,000	$8,400,000	$7,800,000	$7,350,000	$6,000,000	$4,800,000
Profit (Loss)	$ (250,000)	$ 400,000	$ 950,000	$1,450,000	$1,500,000	$1,400,000

simply confirms, that for a given cost structure, a lower price results in a higher break-even point. What is needed is a way to incorporate demand into the chart.

However, it is first necessary to develop price-volume estimates for the alternative prices. At this point, it would be more realistic to develop several demand (volume) estimates for each alternative price. To simplify the illustration here, I have assumed only the most likely volume estimates for each price. Then, for each price-volume estimate, direct production and marketing costs must be estimated. Again, it is important to consider realistic costs which are comparable to costs to be incurred during the product's growth stage. It is also important to avoid the temptation to apportion common costs to the product, since any apportionment is essentially arbitrary. Full cost estimates would be inappropriate because:

(1) Full costs include past costs which are not relevant to the pricing decision;
(2) Overhead absorption rates are poor measures of the opportunity costs of using scarce resources;
(3) Full costs may lead to cost-plus pricing which does not consider demand or competition.

Table 1 shows the type of data that need to be generated. Note that the highest price, $9.00 ($P_6$), is not necessarily the most profitable choice. When the profit and volume data of Table 1 are plotted on the break-even chart for each price, the result is as shown in Exhibit 4. In Exhibit 4, CC is the contribution curve for the new product. The contribution curve shows the relationship between demand (D_1-D_6), direct product profit, total contribution and break-even points for alternative prices. Thus, the analysis has considered the estimated demand function, and the relevant costs for the pricing decision. Exhibit 4 also shows the break-even chart with the capacity constraint.

As the data in Table 1 and Exhibit 4 reveal, the most profitable price is $8.50, with a most likely volume estimate of 1,000,000 units. Frequently, during the introductory stage the firm does not have full production capacity. It may wish to wait until the product has been successively introduced before making additional investments in productive capacity. Suppose that, during the introductory period, the firm has productive capacity for only 900,000 units. Not until price is above $8.50 does

estimated volume go below a million units (Table 1). Therefore, the firm may wish to set the initial price around $9.00. Later, the price may be reduced when (a) additional productive capacity becomes available, (b) competitors begin to enter the market, or (c) price elasticity increases.

The advantage of the product profit-volume analysis is that it allows management to trace the implications of different introductory pricing strategies. For example, if the product is easily imitated by competitors, the firm may wish to pursue a penetration pricing policy, so as to build early high volume and maintain a relatively higher market share in a growing market. In the example given in Table 1, a penetration price of $7.00 yields a short-term profit of $1,000,000 less than the skimming price of $9.00. This $1,000,000 represents a short-term opportunity cost that should be balanced by expected gains due to a higher market share during the growth stage of the product.

Another factor that might influence a penetration pricing policy would be the rate at which the experience factor reduces direct production and marketing costs per unit. For example, if experience could reduce the variable costs to $5.00 per unit, for production of 1,400,000 units or more, then estimated profits for prices $7.00 and $6.50 would be $1,800,000 and $1,250,000, respectively.

Exhibit 4: Break-Even Chart: Price Volume Combinations for New-Product Pricing, Including Capacity Constraints

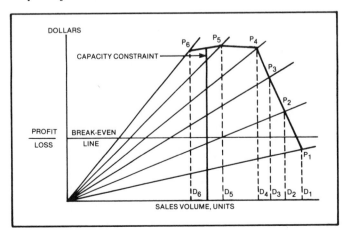

A Strategy Base

In illustrating an approach for pricing new industrial products, my objective has been to show that contribution analysis is adaptable and useful for the pricing task. As I have advocated, pricing strategy must be devised during the product development stage, and both price *and* cost forecasting are important for this purpose. Further, to avoid the common mistake of basing a new product's price on unrealistic introductory production and marketing costs, the experience curve should be utilized to obtain realistic cost estimates.

As demonstrated by the simple illustration, one needs to have proper accounting, financial, and market data when setting prices, as well as information on competitors' prices (actual and expected), cost structures, and capacity utilization; buyers' reactions to price; and the cost structure and corporate objectives of one's own company. Underlying all should be a consistent marketing strategy which includes price. Unless the pricing process is firmly imbedded within a dynamic, long-run marketing strategy, pricing unrelated to the marketing strategy is likely to evolve.

Correct pricing is vital in today's environment, which increases pressures for better, faster, and more frequent pricing decisions. For their guidance, managements need better research information, characterizing the competitive market and customers' responses to prices and to price changes. Also needed are increased budgets for pricing research. The time to worry about market response to a price decision is before the decision has been made.

Critical Trade-Offs

Rodman L. Drake
Managing Director
Cresap, McCormick and Paget Inc.

DECISION MAKERS IN INDUSTRY constantly face trade-off choices. To a general manager, the word trade-off usually means striving for an appropriate balance between short-term profits and longer term strategic objectives. For the manufacturing or operations manager, trade-offs generally focus on cost/benefit analyses, make-or-buy decisions, or material substitutions.

For a marketing or product manager, common trade-offs in ushering products through their life cycles generally focus on such elements of the marketing mix as product reliability, product features, service and technical support, alternative pricing plans, and many more. For instance, a product manager of telecommunications equipment must weigh a customer's "perceived willingness to pay" against the estimated cost of developing and producing a product with desirable but optional features, such as a "self-testing capability."

Ultimately, the product manager may be forced to make a trade-off between the costs and time required to develop the product, and the need to get a product into the marketplace at a price that will be consistent with the needs of the customer and the competitive situation. While these kinds of trade-offs undoubtedly are important to the success of a particular product, they are, in isolation, usually not critical to the development of an overall marketing strategy for a full product line.

On the other hand, they may indeed become critical if a trend develops in the way these trade-offs are made across a number of different products in a product line— if they affect the entire product line, or if they have implications for activities in other functional areas. In these cases, what we have been calling critical trade-offs might also be called strategic trade-offs. The basic point I wish to emphasize is that trade-offs having an impact on an entire product line are, by definition, strategic. Thus, if a trade-off may affect an entire product line, it should be

made in the light of the overall strategy which has been adopted for the product line.

These strategic trade-offs must meet two objectives:
- Maximizing profitability;
- Satisfying the needs of the customer group.

If a critical trade-off is to be considered strategic, it must have long-term implications. That is, it must have the potential for maximizing profitability and/or satisfying customer needs over a longer time span than the current performance period.

With this definition in mind, let us examine how a manager responsible for developing a strategy for an industrial product line identifies areas in which critical trade-offs can be made. Then, we can consider some questions that managers responsible for industrial product lines might ask themselves from time to time to ensure that their trade-off decisions benefit from a strategic perspective.

Identifying Trade-Off Possibilities

To identify opportunities for trade-offs, the individual responsible for a product line must make a fact-based assessment of the company's product line within its industry, taking into consideration both the market and economic trends and the likely competitive forces.

Theoretically, it would seem that an assessment of market, economic, environmental and other factors could lead to a very large number of areas in which strategic trade-offs might be made. In practice, however, the number of areas in which true strategic trade-offs are viable can quickly be reduced to a manageable number by separating structural constraints, or "facts of life," from variables over which management has direct or indirect influence.

Structural constraints are conditions that cannot be altered, or can only be altered slowly over a period of time. They can include both external and internal conditions. For example, external structural constraints might include such factors as the maturity of the industry, economic conditions, the industry's capital intensity, rates of technological change, and so forth. Internal structural constraints might include such factors as the known biases of senior management within the power structure, prolonged limitations of new capital, or commitment to a corporate strategy that favors diversification over rapid expansion of an existing product line.

The variable conditions over which management has some measure of control may be derived from a firm understanding of the structural constraints. These conditions, like the structural constraints, may vary widely. They might include alternative pricing strategies, channels of distribution, or options for providing postpurchase service.

In this approach to the identification of areas for critical trade-offs, it is assumed that basic issues of overall corporate strategy—such as what business the company wishes to be in and what product markets it wishes to serve—have already been decided. Thus, the numerous areas in which a company has to make financial and other trade-offs involving more than one product market have presumably been determined.

As stated earlier, the purpose of identifying the variable areas in which critical trade-offs can be made is to gain a fact-based understanding of the company's product markets, and the economics of each product market, in view of the competitive and environmental situations. This includes understanding how the markets are structured, and what environmental and competitive forces are likely to influence the outlook for a particular product market or business. It is also necessary to understand the economics of the operations of all the participants in a product market, taking into consideration such factors as where value is added, what elasticity costs and margins may have in relation to volume, what commitments have been made to research and development, and so forth.

The overall aim in this analysis is to determine what are the real areas of market and economic strength or vulnerability. In other words, where are the points of leverage and where are the points of vulnerability within a particular product market?

Company X

Exhibits 1 and 2 illustrate some results of a hypothetical analysis of the market and economic strengths and weaknesses of a company we shall call "X," which is in the heavy construction equipment business. Key factors likely to affect the company's long-term market outlook and profitability are shown on each chart.

Exhibit 1: Identifying Areas of Economic and Market Strength for Company X

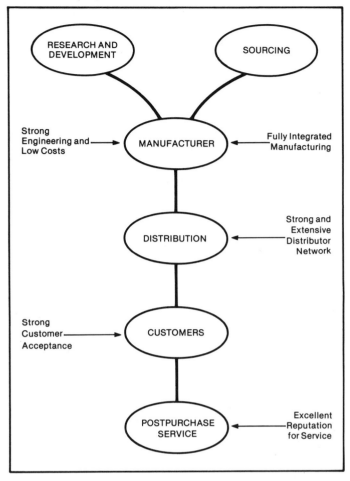

We can infer from these charts that Company X's basic market strategy can be characterized as more or less "follow the leader," or "me-too." That is to say, it is based on strong engineering resources, superior manufacturing efficiency, and tight cost control, as opposed to being a leader in technological innovation. Its strong manufacturing capability has been achieved at least partially because of a long-standing policy of having integrated production facilities at strategic locations throughout the world.

One critical element in the success of this company's strategy is keeping new product introductions and product modifications to a minimum, to avoid disrupting the tightly controlled manufacturing costs. Because new products are based largely on technological advances introduced by competitors, Company X has the ability to copy new designs quickly and get them into its worldwide distribution system. In addition, control of product quality is essential to minimizing any tendency the managers responsible for the field service groups might have to expand their operations. (As the number of complaints grows, field service will want to increase its capacity.)

Exhibit 2: Identifying Areas of Economic and Market Weakness for Company X

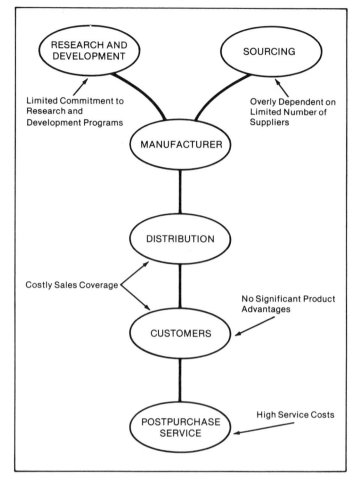

Company X has a strong customer acceptance because of its history of producing reliable equipment, with a strong price and delivery performance. It has built up a strong distributor network throughout the world, which has a reputation for offering a very high level of service. Moreover, the distribution network has been used effectively to gather the competitive intelligence needed to make a "me-too" type of strategy work.

While Company X undoubtedly has a number of significant strengths, it also has certain vulnerabilities. It has yielded the position of being the market leader in new product introduction to its competitors, since it has made only limited commitments to R and D efforts. Also, largely for historical reasons, it has left itself vulnerable to a small number of suppliers of raw materials. The large distribution network it has built up has proved to be expensive in terms of fixed costs, with the result that sales coverage is expensive. Similarly, because of the high costs of the distribution and service network, service costs to customers are higher than those of major competitors. Finally, because of the company's strategy of focusing on product reliability and low manufacturing costs,

customers perceive that Company X's products have no significant advantages over those offered by competitors.

From this analysis, we can deduce that at least one of Company X's major competitors has chosen a different marketing strategy. Specifically, this competitor has made a more research-intensive effort, supported by major development resources, high proximity to the state-of-the-art technology, and a high investment ratio in R and D. The management of this competing company has sought a more direct linkage between R and D and the company's market position. To be successful with its strategy built around technological innovation, this company's requirements differ substantially from those of Company X: The competitor must strive to maintain a delicate balance among R and D, manufacturing and customer service, if it is to be effective. If development becomes too strong, untried or even (conceivably) uneconomic products may be passed on to manufacturing. If this happens, the need to respond to complaints from customers may deter future development work and undermine the basic strategy of technological innovation and superiority. On the other hand, if customer service builds its capabilities to respond to crisis, future development may also suffer as scarce resources are diverted from R and D. In short, this competitor must balance the spheres of influence of R and D, manufacturing and service in a manner quite different from the practices of Company X.

This hypothetical example, involving an analysis of the strengths and vulnerabilities of Company X, and a brief comparison with the situation of one of its competitors, illustrates potential areas for critical trade-offs. Company X's strategy is based on a number of critical trade-offs involving all the principal functional areas: R and D, manufacturing, marketing, and postpurchase service. Certain areas of market and economic strengths identified are structural and can be changed only over a period of time. Other areas are more open to short-term change. Nevertheless, an attempt to influence an accepted market or economic condition usually involves a trade-off that has an effect on more than one function. For instance, a decision to reduce the scope of the distributor network, and/or the services provided, probably would require reconsideration of the "me-too" product introduction strategy. With a weaker distribution network, Company X almost certainly would have to compensate through greater emphasis on innovative product introduction.

Making Trade-Off Decisions

Industrial marketing, unlike consumer marketing, depends heavily on the activities of other functions, such as engineering and development, and manufacturing. This means that market strategy in most such companies is inevitably linked to technological considerations, product design changes, changes in manufacturing costs, or improved service capabilities. It thus differs from consumer marketing strategy, where product positioning, packaging, advertising and point-of-sale promotion are frequently key elements.

Further, although we have advocated a fact-based assessment of market and economic position in a particular product market, such an assessment tends to be more of a subjective judgment in industrial marketing than in consumer marketing. There, sophisticated quantitative measures of market penetration and consumer preference generally are more widely used. Information supporting industrial marketing decisions also lacks the precision of the technical data that top management typically receives from research and development and from manufacturing covering such matters as unit costs, material costs, and the like. Marketing data are quantifiable, but certainly not with the precision of engineering costs based on standards.

Thus, in view of the high degree of interdependence between marketing and other functions, and the lack of precision inherent in many trade-off decisions, there are two questions that managers responsible for implementing a product-line strategy should ask themselves when making trade-off decisions within the framework of an agreed-upon marketing strategy:

- Is the decision consistent with the fact-based assessment of the product markets?
- Does the decision consider fully the impact on other functional areas?

Once a marketing strategy has been agreed upon, the manager responsible for implementing it may be presented with recommendations that seem logical on the surface but, when thought about in terms of the structural conditions or "facts of life," may not represent the best course of action. This often happens when a company is formulating a response to a move made by a competitor. The response obviously must attempt to protect market position and profitability; but it also must not attempt to change market or economic "facts of life," unless this is to be done within an overall strategy aimed at achieving such change over an extended period of time.

Because of the high interdependence of functional areas within an industrial operation, critical trade-offs must not interfere with maintaining an appropriate balance. For instance, in the example involving Company X, the overall strategy is based on an appropriate balance of roles among R and D, manufacturing and marketing. If a trade-off decision is made that does not adequately recognize this balance, it will be counterproductive to the overall strategy. For instance, if marketing starts to respond to competitive moves by requesting more and more product modifications, and this begins to be a recurring theme, one of the traditional market and economic strengths of Company X—the ability to produce a low-priced, highly reliable product—gradually becomes eroded. Similarly, it is not uncommon for operating objectives based on precise numbers generated by manufacturing to have seriously undermined marketing strategies and programs. Such quantitative objectives as "keep the tonnage up," or "maximize the plant loading," frequently fall into this category and, because they are based on hard numbers, they easily get top management attention.

Obviously, the checks and balances in a large industrial concern make it difficult to destroy completely the functional balance built up over the years. Nevertheless, critical trade-offs that do not adequately weigh the need to maintain that balance may lead to costly delays and unnecessary additional coordinative efforts on the part of functional managers. At the extreme, a series of trade-off decisions that does not recognize the linkage with other areas can eventually undermine a sound marketing strategy.

In summary, there are four key points in making trade-off decisions:

- Critical trade-offs in formulating a product-line strategy are not limited to the marketing function; and consequently, by definition, they are really strategic trade-offs.
- The areas for potential trade-offs differ from one company to another, and they can only be identified through a fact-based assessment of each product market.
- The identification of areas for critical trade-offs provides a basis for the development of a sound marketing strategy, and for the development of functional plans and programs to support that strategy.
- Once a marketing strategy has been agreed to, trade-off decisions require an ongoing assessment of known market and economic facts, along with recognition of the need to maintain an appropriate balance among different functional areas, such as research and development, manufacturing and marketing.

The underlying message is this: If you think through your trade-off decisions from a general management perspective, as opposed to a strictly marketing perspective, you will probably avoid the biggest pitfalls.